Essays
on
THOMAS
MANN

Essays
on
THOMAS
MANN

GEORG LUKÁCS

Translated from the German by
STANLEY MITCHELL

The Universal Library
GROSSET & DUNLAP
NEW YORK

Contents

Contents

Translator's Note

In all cases I have used the standard translations for Lukács's quotations from Thomas Mann. Only once or twice have I changed a phrase or word in order to match Lukács's reading of it.

The verse renderings are my own with the exception of the lines on page 46 which are taken from Louis Macneice's translation of *Faust*.

The footnotes are the translator's.

S.M.

Foreword

THESE studies, though put together to form a small book, do not pretend to give an all-round comprehensive picture of Thomas Mann's intellectual and artistic development. They were, of course, intended to throw light on the central problems of his work. The first, in honour of his 70th birthday, tries to elucidate Mann's dialectically complex attitude to the middle class, which, in my opinion, forms the social and hence personal mainspring of his entire career. The second deals with his position vis-à-vis middle class culture and art in his Faust novel and the light it throws on his whole development. The third attempts to relate his style, his affinity with and divergence from contemporary trends to his total outlook. This approach determines the particular emphases of the essays. In a systematic account of Mann's work *Lotte in Weimar* and the Joseph cycle especially, to mention only the most important works, would have had to be dealt with at greater length.

If I have published these essays in one little volume, it was because of subjective and objective reasons which I must briefly explain.

My subjective reason is simply that I can hardly hope now to produce a systematic treatment of Mann's work. Publishing these essays in book form is, therefore, a mark of resignation. And yet I feel justified (subjectively and objectively) in publishing them, painful as the resignation is. Subjectively these essays, despite their incompleteness and essayist character, do sum up discussion in which I have engaged over a lifetime. I was still at school when Mann's writing made its first big impact on me. The *Tonio Kröger* problem (together with Ibsen's epilogue) was a major influence in determining the main lines of my own early work. It was not so much the direct connection, the individual references I made to Mann or even a review of *Royal Highness* (which is published here as an historical document) that were important, as the whole atmosphere in which problems were raised and solutions sought. Mann obviously felt this himself when in a discussion of bourgeois culture he mentioned my book *Soul and Form* (without, to my knowledge, having encountered my youthful essay in Hungarian). He wrote there about his reaction to my arguments: 'We have, I am sure, a particular right to knowledge which we ourselves helped to create merely by our own existence.'

Given our differing reactions to the major events of the time this spiritual closeness was soon to be broken. It had ceased to exist when Mann wrote the lines just quoted: we took up opposite positions vis-à-vis the imperialist First World War. Thomas Mann held the views he described in *Reflections of an Unpolitical Man*; I was drawn to Marxism and joined the Communist Party. It was in this atmosphere that our first and only personal meeting took place. It seems to me that Mann is much too polite and gentle where he describes our opposition in his letter to Seipel: 'I have met Lukács personally. He once spent a whole hour in Vienna propounding his theories to me. While he was talking he was right. Even if the impression he left was an almost hair-raising abstractness. . . .'

This mutual estrangement lasted a long time. It took years for Thomas Mann to get over his wartime views, for his new sense of democracy to make itself felt in his work. It took no less a time for me to integrate myself more and more with the revolutionary working-class movement so that I could outgrow the abstract and sectarian attitudes of my Marxist initiation. This concurrent development laid the basis for my newer, deeper, more objective work on Mann. The essay *Thomas Mann on the Literary Heritage* (*International Literature* 1933) is merely the first milestone of this new argument between us. As I look back on it I realize that it was still too abstract and insufficiently dialectical. (This essay, too, is included here as a document of my development in this question.) The literary battles for a contemporary realism took me further and further into Mann's work. My essays of the late thirties[1] bear the plain traces of this reappraisal.

All this has needed saying to show the reader that I have the right, subjectively, to regard these essays not as occasional pieces put together by kind permission of the publisher but as the résumé (obviously incomplete and essayist in character) of a development which extends over decades. And I hope that this personal history gives objective grounds for treating them as such. For I do not think it was just a personal concern to have seen in the dialectic of art and the bourgeoisie the essence of the early Mann. This formulation is not merely a statement of what the writer Mann was striving to express. Essentially, though of course at that time in embryonic form, it stated a key problem of dying bourgeois culture as a whole, to be seen in Mann's works as much as in my critical analysis of them.

More than four decades have passed since then. We have had two major wars and twelve years of fascism; for over thirty years socialism has existed and grown strong in the Soviet Union. Thomas Mann's path led him over these years from *Tonio Kröger* to the tragedy of Adrian Leverkühn, that of the typical modern bourgeois artist and of typical modern bourgeois art, indissolubly connected with the tragedy of the German people's misdirected development. If today, after three decades of theoretical and practical preoccupation with Marxism, I have attempted to interpret this ideological decay of the bourgeoisie

---

[1] These appeared in the books *Marx and Engels as Literary Historians, The Turning-Point* and *Essays on Realism* which are so far untranslated.

in the work of the last great bourgeois writer, I dare hope objectively that my reflections touch the nub both of Thomas Mann's own work and of the cultural crisis of our time.

Budapest, January 1963.

In Search of Bourgeois Man

Living means fighting within you
The ghosts of dark powers.
Writing is putting on trial
Your inmost self.

Ibsen.

I

IN search of bourgeois man? Is he not to be found everywhere? Is not the culture of the present (at least in the West), from economics right through to literature and music bourgeois? And is not such a question particularly unjustified in the case of Thomas Mann, a writer who from the beginning committed himself to the bourgeoisie and has continued to do so with greater insistence than is customary among writers today.

The question, however, is made more complex by the complete absence of Utopianism in Mann's work (which is not always true of his thought). We intend this descriptively, not as an evaluation. Thomas Mann is a realist whose respect, indeed reverence, for reality is of rare distinction. His detail, still more his plots, his intellectual designs may not stay on the surface of everyday life; his form is quite unnaturalistic. Yet the content of his work never finally leaves the real world. What we are offered in Thomas Mann's work is bourgeois Germany (together with genesis and antecedent paths). And of this we are offered the inner problems, deeply seized, so that while they point dialectically ahead, they do not conjure a Utopian future perspective

13

into a present-day reality. There are not a few great realist works which are shaped in this way. I would mention only Goethe's *Wilhelm Meister* novels. However kindred Mann is to Goethe, here he is his polar opposite.

This re-emphasizes the bourgeois ideal as the guiding principle in Mann's life and work. He is rightly considered the most representative German writer in the first half of our century. A people can, however, be 'represented' by different types of writer. There are 'representative' writers who are prophets of the future, and others whose genius and mission it is to be 'mirrors of the world'. Schiller's urgency and restlessness was just as 'representative' as Goethe's embrace of the moment. But likening Mann to Goethe (or to Balzac or Tolstoy), calling him a 'mirror', still does not tell us what is specific to him.

Goethe's *Meister* novels contain Utopian elements; there are similar features in Balzac, Keller and Tolstoy. We do not find them in Thomas Mann. We are faced then with a special type of 'representative' writer. Thomas Mann presents a complete picture of bourgeois life and its predicaments. But it is a picture of a precise moment, a precise stage of development. (True, this portrait of the German bourgeois of the present only goes up to the period before fascism. So far Mann has not given us a picture of the German as fascist or opponent of fascism). This is why many Germans rediscover themselves so much more deeply, at once more directly and intimately, in Mann's work than in that of other writers. And since the problems are left unanswered, or answered in the most roundabout way, since they are communicated at many levels which are in turn ironically dissolved, the impact of Mann's novels has been much greater than that of his contemporaries. Whatever claims his writing makes on the reader's artistic judgment, whatever the intellectual requirements of his delicately spun web of questions and reservations, his plots and characters are simply and straightforwardly drawn and accessible to the simplest person. And since it is a moral world order that he rejects, the impact is a lasting one. The

14

moments he chooses always mark a particular stage in the development of the German middle class, one to which all who have consciously lived through their own and their country's past will feel themselves perpetually drawn.

This very individual kind of 'representation' deepens with Thomas Mann's slow organic development. Here, too, he is in harmony with the march of reality. Reality, of course, particularly during the second half of Mann's life, was stormy enough, and it was inevitable that this tempo should be reflected in Mann's writing. But this could not affect the epic character of his work as a whole which was rooted in the sensibility of a very leisurely storyteller. The works which reflect these violent upheavals not only remain unflurried, epic and ironical in character—they ripen slowly so that the problems they deal with have already acquired an ideological maturity. These problems are the spiritual and moral pros and cons preceding a particular step forward which history has taken or is about to take. The actual changes are, therefore, omitted. Mann shows only their reflexes in everyday life. But again there must be no confusion between this slow tempo of development and whatever variety of naturalism. Mann's stories never reflect the day-to-day moods of the German middle class. Rather the reverse: as he matured, the more firmly did he oppose the prevailing reactionary trends. But the way in which he countered them, his choice of intellectual weapons once again marks the summit of bourgeois consciousness at the time. Even in opposition Thomas Mann, the creator, never parts company with the bourgeoisie. The extent of his influence reposes on this firm social basis. He is representative in the sense that he symbolizes all that is best in the German bourgeoisie.

This, of course, only refers to the completed work. But this easy, at times almost easy-going, perfection was the outcome of a long and painful struggle with the manifold, above all inner moral problems of a world from which such a work of art could emerge in clear and organic shape. But if Thomas Mann as an artist is the very opposite of the philosopher Schelling who, as Hegel put it, 'undertook his philosophical education in public', if rather his works are rounded summaries of historical stages which have run their course, nevertheless his actual spiritual development necessarily takes place in public.

I believe it wrong to interpret the works of a major writer on the basis of their own theories. If these works are important it is almost always because they achieve a form which can render the conflicts of their times at their fullest range within the given historical reality. Yet these same conflicts pursued in terms of ideas, however fearlessly, can get no further than an honestly stated antithesis which often simply juxtaposes the 'yes' and the 'no' without connection. Sometimes indeed the conflicts may harden into quite false and reactionary positions. But in the best cases this is more than an artistic rounding-off of what the intellect cannot fully seize. It is the corrective which the process of reproducing reality, the passionate pursuit of this process to its very end, *in fine* which reality itself applies to the false thinking of the writer. Nowhere is Balzac's utopian legitimism or Tolstoy's Christian plebeian dream of brotherhood with the peasants more powerfully refuted than in *Le Cabinet des Antiquités* or *Resurrection*.

Thomas Mann is an extreme type of the writer whose greatness lies in being a 'mirror of the world'. Not that he is a philosophical dilettante or an inconsistent thinker. On the contrary he possesses the highest intellectual culture of the bourgeois Germany of his time. Few contemporaries have worked their way so thoroughly through the leading reactionary thinkers of this period, Schopenhauer and Nietzsche. Few have lived out so deeply the relationship between their systems and methods and the crucial problems of the contemporary bourgeoisie. There are few contemporaries where so arduously achieved a philosophical outlook has been made so closely a part of artistic creation.

And this is why the refutation of the wrong-headed, the retrogressive by the very logic of the characters, plots and situations

16

is seldom so manifest as in Thomas Mann. Let me take just one small example: *Buddenbrooks* was written at a time when Thomas Mann, and with him a large section of the German bourgeois intelligentsia, looked to Schopenhauer as the leading spokesman of a German philosophy. For Mann the high road of Germany's intellectual development, and this view persisted a good while after *Buddenbrooks*, led from Goethe via Schopenhauer and Wagner to Nietzsche, and from Nietzsche on to a truly German intellectual culture of the present and future. It is not surprising that Schopenhauer's influence made itself felt in *Buddenbrooks*, that Mann portrayed a Schopenhauerian attitude to life. But how does this appear in the actual work? Thomas Buddenbrook is a broken man, his efforts to revive his firm having long since failed. He has lost hope of his son succeeding him and accomplishing what he has failed to do. His relationship with his wife becomes more and more difficult, intellectually and emotionally. It is at this point that he comes across *The World as Will and Representation*. And what is its effect upon him? 'He was filled with a great surpassing satisfaction. It soothed him to see how a master-mind could lay hold on this strong, cruel, mocking life and enforce and condemn it. His was the gratification of the sufferer who has always had a bad conscience about his sufferings and concealed them from the gaze of a harsh, unsympathetic world, until suddenly, from the hand of an authority, he receives, as it were, justification and license for his suffering—justification before the world, this best of all possible worlds which the master-mind scornfully demonstrates to be the worst of all possible ones! ... He felt that his whole being had unaccountably expanded, and at the same time there clung about his senses a profound intoxication, a strange, sweet, vague allurement which somehow resembled the feelings of early love and longing.' The bitterest opponent of Schopenhauer could not paint a better picture of the philosopher as the apostle of decadence.

We are not concerned at present to examine the way Mann

as thinker looked upon and judged the general problem of decadence at that stage. I gave this example merely to indicate how the intellectual and imaginative questions and answers are separated out in Mann, to justify the methodology of the reflections which follow, that is primarily to concentrate on the works and to interpret Mann the thinker and political man starting from his writing and not, as is customary, the other way round.

II

It is only from this starting-point that the apparent paradox of my first question, the search for bourgeois man as the central problem in Mann and the basis for his popularity and representative position can be meaningfully answered. This question leads us to a fundamental contradiction in the writer's situation in the bourgeois epoch. Friedrich Schiller was the first to define this fundamental tendency of the new bourgeois world by creating the category of 'the sentimental' (the elegiac, satirical and idyllic). Schiller's opposing principles have all the captivating simplicity of a great discovery: 'The writer ... either is nature or he will *seek* her,' he says. It is immediately clear that true realism is the special property of the 'naïve' writer. Schiller illustrates this antithesis very well by contrasting the treatment of a similar episode in Homer and Ariosto.

But complication sets in with a further problem. Schiller himself poses it: is Goethe a 'naïve' writer and, we would add, is not Tolstoy or Mann also one? If the answer is yes, what is Goethe's attitude to modern reality? How does he view the quest for nature, the 'sentimental'? Of small literary figures Schiller was confidently able to say 'that they run wild in their age and are protected by good fortune from its crippling influence'. But it was obvious to him that simple contrasts of this kind were inadequate to define Goethe's position in world literature. It was a little one-sided of him to ask how a 'naïve' writer handles a 'sentimental' theme and then to answer his question with a brilliant exegesis of *Werther*, *Tasso*, *Wilhelm Meister* and *Faust*. Of course Goethe is 'naïve', but for social reasons he is no longer as obviously and uncomplicatedly 'naïve' as Homer. His 'naïveté' is both inborn and with difficulty achieved. It determines his initial approach to, and final shaping of, a theme. But in between the 'sentimental' has run its turbulent course. Hence one may let Schiller's antithesis stand: 'Nature favoured the *naïve* writer with the faculty of acting always as an undivided unity, of being at every moment an independent and complete whole, and of representing humanity in its full extent, as it really was. To the *sentimental* writer she gave the power, or rather instilled the urge, to restore that unity within himself which abstract thought had destroyed, to make humanity complete within himself and to pass from a limited condition to an infinite one.' But in the major realists of the bourgeois epoch, Goethe, Keller, Balzac, Tolstoy, this antithesis appears as a dialectical process, in which the 'sentimental' becomes by realistic handling simply a stage on the way from the original 'naïveté' to the mature.

What, then, is Thomas Mann's position among the great 'naïve' novelists of the nineteenth and twentieth centuries? Our detour was intended to explain the apparent contradiction in our earlier description of him. We called his realism a 'mirror of the world', but also said that he was representative as a conscience of the German middle class. The contradiction is patent, for where a writer embodies conscience, his native 'naïveté' must disappear. The fact of conscience as a force in life gives both expression and acknowledgment to the discrepancy between things as they are and things as they ought to be, between appearance and essence. Have we not got back to Schiller's 'sentimental' writer, to the gulf between ideal and reality? And does this not dispose of the 'naïve' realism of the epic tradition? We think not. What should be, need not, as in Kant and, for the most part, in Schiller, oppose itself to a differently ordered real world, but can in a Hegelian way emerge from the contradictory identity of appearance and essence. Conscience then is simply the injunction: 'Become what you are; be your essence, develop the essential, living core within you, whatever the disruptive influences of the inner and outer world.'

It is in this sense that the deeply and consciously bourgeois Thomas Mann is conscience for the German middle class. One could put it that the sociological core of Schiller's discovery of the essence of modern art becomes conscious in Mann. His overriding conviction is that to enquire into the essence of bourgeois man today is to ask what it is to be a bourgeois. The search for bourgeois man threw open to him all the questions concerning the present and future and the culture of our time.

One of Goethe's great successors, Gottfried Keller, wrote an impressive *oeuvre* round this question. But this was in the conditions of mid-nineteenth-century Switzerland. Thomas Mann saw the deep difference (though not at the beginning of his career). In the twenties he said about Switzerland: 'We have before us an offshoot of the German people, which, at an early stage, broke away from the main body and shared its intellectual and moral experiences only to a limited degree. But it never lost contact with Western European thought and did not undergo the Romantic degeneration which turned us into solitaries and outlaws. . . . But one thing the Swiss phenomenon can teach us is not to confuse a stage in Germany's history, which though mistaken was inevitable, with the essence of Germany itself. . . .'

Inevitably Mann did not start out from such insights which only the First World War and Germany's defeat vouchsafed him. But then they are not quite so simple and unsociological as Mann himself sometimes imagined them. During the War he wrote about his early work: 'It is true that I rather slept through the transformation of the German burgher into a bourgeois . . .' He underestimates here his own achievement. One need only take the contrast between the development of the Hagenström and Buddenbrook families: the Hagenströms are a perfect illustration of that development of burgher into bourgeois which Mann says he 'slept through'. So little did he 'sleep through' this development that the second half of his first novel, from a sociocultural and moral point of view, turns on the question: who really represent the middle class, the Hagenströms or the Buddenbrooks?

Superficially the answer is simple. The patrician culture of the Buddenbrooks is doomed and the Hagenströms rule the new Germany. So much is clear; and Mann did not 'sleep through' it. Nor did he resign himself to it. Had he done so, he would have had to renounce the idea of a contemporary German culture and literature. He would have become a *laudator temporis acti*, a new Raabe.[1]

Instead the question faces him: who is the bourgeois? What does his type look like, what is its pattern and culture if he does not belong with the victorious Hagenströms? In this light the Buddenbrooks appear not simply as a family on the downgrade but, despite their decadent tinges, as upholders of a bourgeois culture which was once Germany's pride and could still be the source of its resurgence, could provide an organic continuation of the glorious past. In this sense the Buddenbrooks saga is the story of what happens to Germany's cultural traditions in the nineteenth century.

Mann's first novel rests on a double contrast. Beside the opposition between the Hagenströms and Buddenbrooks there is the internal opposition between Thomas and Christian Buddenbrook. Between Thomas and Christian the question is whether to surrender to decadence or fight it. The character of Christian (like that of the hero of the story *The Bajazzo*) shows how the modern world, with its break-up of the old patrician bourgeoisie, has thoroughly destroyed the old morality. The type of the turn of the century, the *fin-de-siècle* has its ancestor here: the personality which destroys itself by undermining these bourgeois principles of life which have shaped it—fulfilment of duty, choosing a career.

[1] Wilhelm Raabe (1831-1910), a provincial German novelist.

21

The same corrosive forces are also at work in Thomas but he keeps them in check through stern self-discipline. Where Christian goes to pieces as a person Thomas forms for himself a bourgeois personality. Yet the source of this form, outer and inner, is despair; he recoils from emotional anarchy and disintegration. 'At last he (Thomas, G. L.) said, and his voice had a ring of feeling, "I have become what I am because I did not want to become what you are. If I have inwardly shrunk from you, it has been because I needed to guard myself—your being, and your existence, are a danger to me—that is the truth." '

This is the 'composure' of Thomas Buddenbrook which becomes the aesthetic and ethic of a new bourgeois culture. Does this mean that Mann has found his bourgeois? No, alas! Thomas is brother to Christian in spirit, too. He has become the good bourgeois by doing violence to his own nature. When he fails with his first and only attempt to participate in the new economic development of the bourgeoisie, the Hagenström path, he becomes more and more a figurehead, acting out his life— and Thomas Mann underscores this with irony.

Is this bourgeois man? The question stays in the balance. In a conversation with his sister, Thomas quotes a remark of his wife's about Christian: 'There's nothing of the burgher about Christian. Thomas—he's even less of a burgher than you yourself.' His sister is shocked and answers: 'Burgher, Tom? What did she mean? Why, it seems to me there is no better burgher on top of the earth than you are!' Thomas demurs: 'Oh, well— she didn't mean it just in that sense. . . .'

But this does not resolve Mann's dilemma of 'composure' or emotional anarchy. In fact only now does the question take a central place in his pre-First World War writings; especially in *Tonio Kröger* and *Death in Venice*, stories about artists, where the problem is the life of the artist himself. That is, can one by restraining the emotions, by a policy of 'composure' turn artistic activity into a career? Mann here takes artistic activity as a symbol for any kind of genuine culture, for any profession or career that comes from within. Of the import of his hero he says in *Death in Venice*: 'Gustav Aschenbach was the poet spokesman of all those who labour at the edge of exhaustion; of the overburdened, of those who are already worn out but still hold themselves upright; of all our modern moralizers of accomplishment, with stunted growth and scanty resources, who yet contrive by skilful husbanding and prodigious spasms of will to produce, at least for a while, the effect of greatness. There are many such, they are the heroes of the age.' In these words Mann reveals his own impact at the time.

So far so good. Did this mean he had found his bourgeois? The Russian painter, Lisaveta Ivanovna, calls her friend Tonio Kröger a 'bourgeois run astray'. And Tonio himself sees clearly on the one hand that a real art (a real culture and morality) could only be achieved in his day by taking the path he had chosen. On the other hand he loves life and rates it higher than an art forced to stand aside from life. His description of life is very bourgeois: 'Don't think of Caesar Borgia or any drunken philosophy that has him for a standard bearer. He is nothing to me, your Caesar Borgia. I have no opinion of him, and I shall never comprehend how one can honour the extraordinary and daemonic as an ideal. No, life as the eternal antimony of mind and art does not represent itself to us as a vision of savage greatness and ruthless beauty; we who are set apart and different do not conceive it as, like us, unusual; it is the normal, respectable, and admirable that is the kingdom of our longing; life, in all its seductive banality!' We seem once more to have reached our goal. It is ordinary people like Hans Hansen and Ingeborg Holm who constitute bourgeois life. They do—in the dreams of Tonio and his kind. But if this discovery was anything more than a lyrical irony, Thomas Mann would have had to give up all idea of a bourgeois culture. For the Hans Hansens and Ingeborg Holms have no more relevance to the cultural development of the German middle class from Goethe to Thomas Mann than the

Hagenströms or the Klöterjahns, though they are considerably more attractive to look at, which fits them better as the objects of a dream. But even the most sincere of dreams is deceptive. In Mann's *Fiorenza* the dying Lorenzo di Medici says to Savonarola. 'Whither the longing urges, there one is not, that one is not—you know? And yet man likes to confuse himself with his longing.'

So it would seem after all that the 'bourgeois run astray', Tonio Kröger, Thomas Buddenbrook's soul-mate become writer, and the genuine bourgeois with his code of 'composure', embody the true ethic of the new bourgeoisie. But Mann again passes ruthless judgment on himself. *Death in Venice* shows this. For what was but dream and tendency in *Tonio Kröger* Gustav Aschenbach brings to full flower. He creates a perfectly formed life and an impressive body of work on the basis of a 'composure' ethic. Both life and work rise above the vulgar everyday with a stern pride, above both its small-minded philistinism and its equally small-minded anarchist bohemianism. But it takes only a little conflict, provoked by scarcely anything tangible, and a dream within this conflict, for the 'composure' to break hopelessly, irresistibly down, as if it had never been the product of a sincere, self-denying, hard-won life. 'That night he had a fearful dream—if dream be the right word for a mental and physical experience which did indeed befall him in deep sleep, a thing quite apart and real to his senses, yet without seeing himself as present in it. Rather its theatre seemed to be his own soul, and the events burst in from outside, violently overcoming the proud resistance of his spirit; passed through him and left him, left the whole cultural structure of a lifetime trampled on, ravaged and destroyed.'

This self-judgment forms the balance-sheet of Mann's pre-war work. One should not be led by the happy, comedy ending of *Royal Highness* to underestimate this deeply pessimistic irony. The fate of the hero here is in any case bathed in an atmosphere of fairytale improbability and quite pronouncedly presented as an unparadigmatic exception. On the other hand this second novel is as much a postscript to *Buddenbrooks* as a prologue to *Death in Venice*. In Prince Albrecht the formalism of 'composure' dissolves into the self-awareness of its emptiness and triviality. He compares himself and his royal 'composure' with the behaviour of a halfwit who thinks he is signalling departing trains to depart: 'But "the Hatter" deludes himself into thinking that his waving sends the train off. That's like me. I wave, and the train starts. But it would start without me, and my waving makes no difference, it's mere silly show. I'm sick of it . . .' And Dr. Unterbein, tutor to the main character, an enthusiastic advocate of 'composure' and the excellent qualities which should spring from it, collapses like Aschenbach—as the result of a tiny unimportant happening. 'The quarrelsome and uncongenial man . . . who had haughtily resisted familiarity, and had ordered his life cold-bloodedly with a view to results alone . . . there he lay now: the first hitch, the first obstacle in the field of accomplishment, had brought him to a miserable end.'

One should not take this just as a secondary or indeed peripheral question of bourgeois culture in pre-First World War Germany. It touches the very centre: the ethic of 'composure' is most intimately connected with the spiritual lives of the finest figures, the most sincere intellectuals in the cultural world of Wilhelmine (imperialistically Prussianized) Germany. For intellectuals—notably for those who were not out to seek their fortunes in the Hagenström fashion—the choice between Christian and Thomas Buddenbrook, between emotional anarchy and 'composure', was extremely typical. (Let me note in passing that some of the leading sociologists amongst Mann's contemporaries did their best to Buddenbrookize and Aschenbachize the Hagenström path in a moral and socio-cultural manner. This applies especially to Rathenau, Max Weber and Troeltsch.) The fact that a philosophy of 'composure' led logically to Prussianism emerges very clearly from Mann's own development. It was no accident that the writer-hero of *Death in Venice* had earned fame by writing an epic on Frederick the Great; he was foreshadowing his creator's work in the First World War. But Mann the artist occupies a peculiar and paradoxical position here. On the one hand he showed that the way out of the Christian-Thomas Buddenbrook dilemma led to accepting Germany's Prussianization; yet artistically he subjected the whole ethic of 'composure' to a withering critique, exposing its worthlessness and unreality.

In this he was continuing the work of Fontane's old age. Fontane, too, even more positively than the maturing Mann, admired and praised Prussian behaviour codes, Prussian military heroes, the Prussian 'conquest' of the wretchedness of bourgeois life. But artistically, in *Schach von Wuthenow, Irrungen Wirrungen* and *Effi Briest*, the same Fontane castigates this type without mercy. Yet more than personal sympathies bound Fontane to him. In life, beset by all manner of doubt, he often saw in him a moral way out of the inhuman human predicaments of his time. Fontane and Mann were the first and only German writers to unmask the inner weakness of the Prussian behaviour ethic (in which connection I would draw attention to that little grotesque *The Railway Accident*).

III

Such was Mann's deep ideological predicament as he, reflecting the development of his country, entered the First World War. His situation, looking back on it from the vantage-point of today, was paradoxical to an extreme. The outbreak of this national crisis found both Mann's artistic critique of the Prussian ethic as well as his personal and political attachment to it at their height. And for the historian looking back with prophetic hindsight it is extremely surprising to see how little Mann understood the real achievements of his development and how passionately he drew the wrong conclusions from his work.

But platonic wonder at such a contradiction in a thinking man must give place to a problem, to a task of understanding.

26

This is not, of course, to defend Mann's war writings. If, as still happens in England and America, later works like *The Magic Mountain* are interpreted in the light of the *Reflections of an Unpolitical Man*, the result will inevitably be a reactionary distortion. The problem is rather to realize that Mann's political aberration in the First World War was no accidental stage in his 'search for bourgeois man', but a necessary phase in the disastrous development of German ideology as a whole.

Up to now we have examined the problems in Mann's work as they were actually portrayed. What, however, was their social basis? (Not that Mann was aware of this at the time.) Some ten years after the First World War Mann excellently described the attitude of most of the best German intellectuals towards the political and social condition of their country. He was writing of Richard Wagner: 'His participation in the '48 cost him twelve years of torment and exile; later, repenting of his "abandoned" optimism, in face of the *fait accompli* of Bismarck's empire, he minimized his share in it as best he could with the realization of his dream. He went the way of the German bourgeoisie: from the revolution to disillusionment, to pessimism and a resigned, power-protected inwardness.'

This attitude of 'power-protected inwardness' has a long history behind it, with deep roots in the poverty of Germany's political development. I must briefly touch on it here since it throws a special light, not only on the path of Mann himself, but also on his relationship to the German middle class.

To summarize: apart from exceptional figures like Lessing, the whole of German classical literature and philosophy operated in an atmosphere of 'power-protected inwardness'. True, German writers and thinkers found this power—the semi-feudal absolutism of the petty principalities—deeply problematic and often downright alien. But when Napoleon's wars of conquest thrust a real power onto the scene which threatened political and social reform, the best Germans fiercely divided. Goethe and Hegel opted for Napoleon and wished to see the whole of Germany turned into a Confederation of the Rhine. The *Phenomenology of Mind*, completed at the time of the Battle of Jena, makes the French Revolution and the new bourgeois society it had created the climax of modern history and allots to the Germans the task of constructing an ideology appropriate to the new conditions—i.e. 'power-protected inwardness' plus the guarantee of those political and social reforms which Napoleon, the 'great constitutional lawyer', as Hegel later called him, was to introduce, against the wishes of the princes of the Rhine Confederation.

There is no need to waste time today pointing out the Utopianism of this conception. Goethe's views were very similar. The idea that Napoleonic France could permanently stabilize its hegemony over Europe without awakening a desire for freedom among the peoples whom it had purged of their feudal dross was pure Utopianism. The very purging would arouse their national awareness. It was equally Utopian to imagine that Germany could assume ideological leadership of this new world without even trying to become politically independent.

However, it was no more unrealistic than the dreams of the honest Prussian reformers who for their part hoped to implement the achievements of the French Revolution (at least partially) simply by liberating Prussia from Napoleon's yoke and leaving Germany itself undisturbed. They imagined they could abolish the social foundations and political consequences of Prussian feudal absolutism without getting rid of the Junkers and the Hohenzollerns. And the 'power-protected inwardness' of Romanticism which sprang from Napoleon's defeat showed only too clearly what a wretched thing this broken Utopia had been. Here then Utopia was ranged against Utopia, mirroring the inability of Germany's ideologists to be anything more than spectators (or pretty ineffective actors) in the drama of their country's destiny. This 'artistic period'[1] continued up to the 1830

---

[1] *Kunstperiode*: "period of art"—Heine's term for the contemplative ethos of the Goethe period.

July Revolution in France. A more realistic course of development set in from this date but was cut short by the tragedy of 1848 and then the tragi-comedy of 1870. In 1848 the Germans really did have the choice of freeing themselves democratically or of retaining their political poverty. In 1870 the intellectuals capitulated once more to the power of the Prussianized German Reich, inevitably a reactionary creation.

Thus the German intellectuals, as Mann rightly wrote of Wagner, continued to live in a state of 'power-protected inwardness'. But history never repeats itself; similarities are more often formal than real. Hence we must distinguish between the 'power-protected inwardness' of Goethe under Napoleon's Confederation of the Rhine and of Thomas Mann during Wilhelmine imperialism. In all essential respects Goethe's outlook was progressive; but it was Mann's fate to be born into the age of decadence, with its peculiar ambience in which one could transcend the decadence only by imaginatively realizing its extreme moral consequences. Further, Goethe's attitude to Napoleon's power involved no obligation to defend reactionary tendencies, no objective conflict of loyalties. But the outbreak of the First World War turned the situation of Mann and the German middle class inside out: 'inwardness' had now to become the ideological shield of 'power', in other words reactionary Prussian-German imperialism.

Hence, Mann's paradoxical and near-tragic situation in the First World War. But as an artist he could not cease looking for bourgeois man. He wished to seize the predicament of the German bourgeois at its core, to listen for the contradictions between being and consciousness and chart their future course. This alone, to quote Schiller on Goethe, was 'a great and truly heroic idea'; and even the greatest of men need not feel ashamed at having made mistakes in such a venture, especially as in this case they were not subjective and personal, but arose out of Mann's deep involvement with Germany which included the many centuries of political poverty.

Thomas Mann was, therefore, quite right, a few years later, to describe his wartime book in this way: 'It was bent on being a monument; if I mistake not it has become one. It was a rearguard action, in the grand style—the latest and last of German middle class romanticism; fought in the full consciousness that it was a lost cause and thus not without greatness of soul; fought indeed, with insight into the mental unhealthiness and viciousness of all sympathy with the *fey*; yet also, it is true, with aesthetic, too aesthetic contempt of health and virtue, which were felt—and scorned—as the sum and essence of that before which one retreated fighting: politics, democracy.'

The passage is an accurate autobiographical commentary. To place it correctly in the wider framework of German history, it must, however, be studied as it was meant to be—from the standpoint of Mann's further development. It was *only* because his rearguard action was followed by an advance towards democracy that it was 'not without greatness of soul'. If someone today were desperately to defend a hopelessly (and rightly) lost cause, to cling to a doomed past without believing in its right to prevail, then he would not only condemn himself to a comic, unintentional quixotry, an empty stance of 'composure'. His sad chivalry would turn into nihilist hypocrisy; his retreat be but a preliminary to the assault of a revived reactionary barbarism, a wanton attempt to burn down the new and restore the buried past to a brief vampire-like existence upon a Golgotha of civilization. Mann's noble farewell to the more than problematic past of his country was, in contrast to such tendencies, a real farewell. It opened up a new path, the path to democracy.

IV

Mann's conversion to democracy during the post-war years was the outcome of a great national crisis. Yet though it came as a turning-point, a decisive change in his personal development, it was by no means unprepared, surprising as this may seem to the superficial observer. It emerged from the inner dialectic of the path he had been following. He now takes a new attitude to his sought-for bourgeois. The difference between the pre-war and wartime Thomas Mann and the best of his fellow-Germans is 'simply' that he experienced more deeply and followed through more radically the problems which affected them all. Nevertheless, his intellectual and spiritual origins are the same, which is why even the most outlandish of his works has a familiar quality which his fellow-Germans could recognize. When Mann placed his early work by citing the names of Platen, Storm and Nietzsche, he characterized this peculiar situation in a very precise manner. In the rigour of its content and form a solitary *oeuvre*, his work rose from the very midst of the plain it dominated; it incorporated heights and lowlands.

This relationship altered radically with Mann's ideological and political change of heart after the war. The German bourgeois now pursues quite a different path from the questing writer. The ideological baggage salvaged by the Germans from the collapse of their first attempt at world conquest was the 'front-line experience' and the hope that they might try once again, with improved methods, to bring off what had eluded them. One method was a more thorough clearing-out of democracy. Thomas Mann, however, not only broke completely and wholeheartedly with German imperialism; he not only grasped the importance of democracy for the rebirth of a truly German culture (during the War he still spurned democracy as un-German). He also saw the connection between the ideology and sensibility of decadence and the previous development of Germany. From now on he regards the struggle for democracy as a struggle against decadence. This view takes his war book forward in a fruitfully paradoxical way. In the latter he had bundled together decadence, a sympathy for disease and decay, night and death with his defence of the German war-effort. But this defence became so deeply enmeshed in the bewildering tangle of pros and cons, that at the end of his frenzied attempt to justify German decadence he saw himself convinced of the sole rightness of the contrary principle. The events of 1918 assisted him.

It is education which now moves into the forefront of Mann's writing. But we must ask again whether this did not mean the end of his *faculté maîtresse*, his peculiar genius: the anti-Utopian nature of his talent? Yes and no. And rather more no than yes. For the mature Thomas Mann is an educator *sui generis*. And what makes him this is not only the ironic reservations with which he tells a story or the good-humoured balance he maintains in composition. These give expression to a deeper connection, a more important meaning. He is not the kind of educator who wants to impart to his pupils a lesson from the outside, however well thought-out, however right. He is an educator in the Platonic sense of anamnesis: the pupil himself should discover the new idea within him, and bring it to life.

As the educator of his people, Mann now looks for his bourgeois in a more exploratory way. His search has found a concrete content. He seeks the spirit of democracy in the mind of the German bourgeois, tracking down the newest hints and signs in order to awaken and foster them in fictional form. He tries to implant them not as an alien idea, but as something which the reader discovers in himself, something sought for and at last found.

This is more or less the reason why Mann stood so alone in the Weimar Republic. Just as the reforms of Stein and Scharnhorst were inspired not by a popular movement in Prussia but by Prussia's defeat at the Battle of Jena, so German democracy after 1918 was not something that had been striven and fought for, but the—unwelcome as it appeared—gift of an adverse destiny. Thus the newborn democracy, which never really took root, had bitter enemies, opportunistic time-servers, and few real friends and supporters. And these mostly accepted it as an offering from Heaven, making not the slightest attempt to link it up with German history which they had in any case revised. In a word, Thomas Mann's isolated position during the Weimar democracy was the result of his search for such connections. As an educator he was looking for a sense of democracy sprung from a German ethos. This is why he was the only bourgeois writer of this period for whom democracy became a matter of *Weltanschauung*, and a problem of German *Weltanschauung* in particular.

Hence the struggle for German democracy is put into a wide philosophical frame. It is the struggle of light and darkness, day and night, health and sickness, life and death. And Thomas Mann, so intimately tied to Germany's past, sees clearly as an artist that he was resuming an age-old battle of German ideology. We need only go back to Goethe's attitude to the Romantics: 'Classical I call what is healthy, Romantic what is sick,' he said, rejecting Kleist as a 'body with which Nature intended well but which has been struck by an incurable disease.' Now when in *The Magic Mountain* the spokesman of the reactionary, Fascist, anti-democratic *Weltanschauung*, the Jesuit Naphta, sets out his ideas, he does so almost in the words of Novalis: 'On the contrary, Naphta hastened to say. Disease was very human indeed. For to be man was to be ailing. Man was essentially ailing, his state of unhealthiness was what made him man. There were those who wanted to make him "healthy", to make him "go back to nature", when the truth was, he had never been "natural" ... the whole Rousseauian paraphernalia had as its goal nothing but the dehumanization, the animalization of man.... In man's spirit, then, resided his true nobility and his merit—in his state of disease, as it were, in a word, the more ailing he was, by so much was he the more man. The genius of disease was more human than the genius of health.'

We see that a decisive change has occurred in Mann's outlook. Yet however firmly he takes the side of democracy against the specifically German decadence which sprang from a reactionary social backwardness; and however impressive, well-modulated, deeply thought-out the literary forms he finds for his new outlook, he fails as a thinker to realize that, objectively, his new stage of development marks a break with the teachers of youth, Schopenhauer and Nietzsche. He does, of course, see connections of this kind. What he writes about Hamsun could not be bettered: 'My great colleague, Knut Hamsun, for example, in Norway, although an old man now, is an ardent Fascist. He makes propaganda for this party in his own country and has not been ashamed publicly to jeer at a world-famous victim of German Fascism, the pacifist Ossietzky. This is, of course, not the behaviour of an old man who has stayed young in heart. It is the behaviour of a writer of the 1870 generation whose formative literary influences were Dostoyevsky and Nietzsche and who has not moved from the anti-liberal apostasy fashionable at the time. He does not understand what is really happening today and does not realize that he is compromising his talent irretrievably by his political—or I should say his human—behaviour.' But such insights did not stop Mann from wanting to preserve Nietzsche for the world of democratic ideas.

Yet in his creative work Mann was much more definite. The important novel *The Magic Mountain* is devoted to the ideological struggle between life and death, health and sickness, reaction and democracy. With his usual symbolic flair Mann sets these struggles in a Swiss luxury sanatorium. Here then sickness and health, their psychological and moral consequences are not abstract theorems, they are not 'symbolic' in a narrow sense, but grow organically and directly out of the physical, mental and emotional lives of the people living there. Only someone who read the book superficially at the time of its publication could have missed the political and philosophical problems which underlay the rich and fascinating picture of physical illness. A closer look shows that it is just such a *milieu* which can bring out all the dialectical aspects of the problem. But the seclusion of life in the sanatorium has yet a more important artistic function. Mann, like most really good novelists, worries little about details of characterization. He rarely 'invents' them. But he had

an infallible instinct for the right kind of story and surroundings, that which would most clearly bring out his particular
problem, which would give most scope for pathos and irony.
There is always a delightful mingling in his work of a phantastic or semi-phantastic whole and very down-to-earth detail.
Thomas Mann was following on here from Chamisso (*Peter Sch-
lemihl*), E. T. A. Hoffmann and Gottfried Keller, but in an altogether original way. Neither in technique nor in use of detail
did he resemble them. 'We describe the everyday,' he once said,
'but the everyday becomes strange if it is cultivated on strange
foundations.' The small princely court of *Royal Highness* produced just such a semi-phantastic background to the problem
of 'composure'. The sanatorium in *The Magic Mountain* does the
same.

The characters are 'on holiday', removed from everyday cares
and the struggle for existence. The whole mental, emotional,
moral world which they bring with them has a chance to express itself more freely, uninhibitedly, more concentratedly, to
open out to the ultimate questions of life. What emerges is a
deeply realistic portrayal of the contemporary bourgeois which
has its tragi-comic distortions and its moments of phantasy. The
inner emptiness, the moral instability knows no bounds and
often explodes in the most grotesque forms. On the other hand,
the better exemplars become aware of a meaning to life of
which they have had no time to think in the everyday world
of capitalism.

These are the conditions for the 'educational novel' which
deals with an average pre-War German, Hans Castorp. Its main
intellectual theme is the symbolical duel between the representatives of light and darkness, the Italian humanist democrat Settembrini and the Jesuit-educated Jew, Naphta, spokesman of a
Catholicising, pre-Fascist ideology. These two wage war over the
soul of an average German bourgeois.

It is alas impossible in the small compass of these remarks to
give any real indication of the richness of these duels, which are

intellectual, human, emotional, political, moral and philosophical. We must limit ourselves to the fact that they end in a draw. Hans Castorp, exhausted by his efforts to reach clarity in his political and philosophical thinking, sinks into the mean, mindless, repellent everyday life of the Magic Mountain. For the 'holiday' from material cares has two sides. It may raise one intellectually, but it may also push one down further into the morass of the instincts than would normally have been possible in everyday life 'down below'. People do not gain any new and better faculties in this rarified, half-phantastic milieu. But the faculties they do have acquire much greater definition. Objectively their inner potentialities are not increased. But we see them unartificially through a magnifying glass, in slow motion. It is true that in the end Castorp 'saves' himself from complete submergence by joining the German army in August, 1914. But from the standpoint of German intelligentsia and bourgeoisie, of all those who stood at a crossroads, yet could come to no decision in their 'power-protected inwardness', participation in the war, in word or deed, was, as Ernst Bloch once wittily put it, just 'one more long holiday'.

Thomas Mann's account, then, of the effect of his own new outlook on the mind of the German bourgeois is as sceptical, and justifiably so, as his critique of the anti-democratic ideology is firm. Both themes are developed in the Novelle Mario and the Magician. In between, in Disorder and Early Sorrow, Mann gives a nuanced ironical picture of the melancholy preoccupation with death of a typical bourgeois of the pre-war period, who feels intellectually, emotionally and morally forsaken in the Weimar republic, although he is vaguely aware that his attitude is deeply problematic. 'He knows,' Mann wrote of Cornelius, 'that professors of history do not like history for what it is but for what it has been. They hate upheavals in the present because they feel them to be lawless, incoherent and impudent —in a word "unhistorical". Their heart belongs with the coherent, pious and historical past.... What has passed is eternal, that is, it is dead. And death is the source of all piety and all traditional values.'

The later *Novelle* is *Mario*, written in the Weimar years. The story takes place in Italy, which is no accident since what we are concerned with here is the mass tactics of fascism, the use of suggestion and hypnosis. The assault on the intellect and the will—this is what the philosophy of militant reaction comes to once it leaves the study and the literary cafés for the streets, when the Schopenhauers and Nietzsches are succeeded by the Hitlers and Rosenbergs. Thomas Mann gives this new phase once more a tangible presence. Again he presents a subtle spectrum of all the different kinds of helplessness with which the German bourgeois faces the hypnotic power of fascism. And again we must content ourselves with one significant example.

A 'gentleman from Rome' refuses to submit to the magician's hypnotic command to dance, only to succumb after a short but tough resistance. Thomas Mann adds a penetrating account of this defeat: 'If I understand what was going on, it was the negative character of the young man's fighting position which was his undoing. It is likely that *not* willing is not a practical state of mind; *not* to want to do something may be in the long run a mental content impossible to subsist on. Between not willing a certain thing and not willing at all, in other words yielding to another person's will, there may lie too small a space for the idea of freedom to squeeze into.' The defencelessness of those German bourgeois who did not want Hitler but who obeyed him for over a decade without demur has never been better described. But what is the reason for this defencelessness?

V.

On one occasion Hans Castorp says of Settembrini, the democrat, 'You are a windbag and a hand-organ man to be sure. But you mean well, you mean much better, and more to my mind than that knife-edged little Jesuit and terrorist, apologist of the Inquisition and the knout, with his round eye-glasses—though he is nearly always right when you and he come to grips over my paltry soul, like God and the Devil in the medieval legends. . . .' Why can Naphta conquer Settembrini in argument? The question receives a clear answer in the novel. At one point, when Castorp is ill, he has a conversation with his tutor in democracy about the capitalist world 'down below'. Castorp sums up his own gloomy moral experience in these words: 'One must be rich down there . . . if you aren't rich, or if you leave off being, then woe be unto you . . . it often struck me that it was pretty strong, as I can see now, though I am a native of the place and for myself have never had to suffer from it. . . . What were the words you used—phlegmatic and energetic. That's very good. But what does it mean? It means hard, cold. And what do hard and cold mean? They mean cruel. It is a cruel atmosphere down there, cruel and ruthless. When you lie here and look at it, from a distance, it makes you shudder.' But Settembrini calls all this sentimentality best left to the 'drones'. He is a harbinger of progress *sans phrase*. He makes no self-criticism, has neither doubts nor reservations, which is why—although he has no personal stake in it—he is such an uncritical standard-bearer of the capitalist system. And that is why he has no really effective intellectual weapons with which to fight Naphta's anti-capitalist demagogy. This brings out perfectly the basic weakness of the average modern bourgeois democratic attitude when faced with a reactionary anti-capitalist demagogy. At the same time it reveals Castorp's own indecision and unwillingness to act, the same pure negativity that we saw in the unavailing resistance of the 'gentleman from Rome'.

Thomas Mann also shows us in his hero the inner social mechanism of the modern German bourgeois psyche. He says of Hans Castorp: 'A man lives not only his personal life, as an individual, but also, consciously or unconsciously, the life of his epoch and his contemporaries. He may regard the general, impersonal foundations of his existence as definitely settled and taken for granted, and be as far from assuming a critical attitude toward them as our good Hans Castorp really was; yet it is quite conceivable that he may none the less be vaguely conscious of the deficiencies of his epoch and find them prejudicial to his own moral well-being. All sorts of personal aims, ends, hopes, prospects, hover before the eyes of the individual, and out of these he derives the impulse to ambition and achievement. How, if the life about him, if his own time seem, however outwardly stimulating, to be at bottom empty of such food for his aspiration; if he privately recognize it to be hopeless, viewless, helpless, opposing only a hollow silence to all the questions man puts, consciously or unconsciously, yet somehow puts, as to the final, absolute, and abstract meaning in all his efforts and activities; then, in such a case, a certain laming of the personality is bound to occur, the more inevitably the more upright the character in question; a sort of palsy, as it were, which may even extend from his spiritual and moral over into his physical and organic part. In an age that affords no satisfying answer to the eternal question of "Why?" "To what end?" a man who is capable of achievement over and above the average and expected modicum must be equipped either with a moral remoteness and single-mindedness which is rare indeed and of heroic mould, or else with an exceptionally robust vitality. Hans Castorp had neither the one nor the other of these; and thus he must be considered mediocre, though in an entirely honourable sense.'

In the novel—the quotation occurs near the beginning and traces the previous development of the engineer, who has just graduated—this mediocrity born of the lack of worthwhile aims may indeed be most honourable, even if with a little irony. But when the Castorp type is confronted by the life-and-death questions of his country, he must be judged differently, just as his situation is different. His honourable mediocrity, his apathy, indecision, his powerlessness before Naphta's demagogy, despite his sympathy with Settembrini, are all transformed into historical guilt. The 'gentleman from Rome' was also honourable in his desire to 'fight for the dignity of the human race', but this did not save him. He joined in with the rest of the bacchantes who had yielded up their wills to the fascist hypnosis. And this wild dance was within an ace of becoming the death dance of civilization.

If, therefore, Thomas Mann had really found his German bourgeois in Professor Cornelius, Hans Castorp or the 'gentleman from Rome'; or, rather, if his search had stopped with his masterly portrait of the German bourgeois who tolerated Hitlerism and even took part in its unscrupulous wars and plundering expeditions 'as a good honest soldier',[1] then his works would have ended on a note of pessimism, deeper than that of any other German writer.

It is, therefore, no accident that during the fearful years of Hitler's rule, while the German people degenerated under fascism, Mann wrote his one great historical work, *Lotte in Weimar* (1939). In the giant figure of Goethe he brought together all the best forces in the German bourgeoisie. Goethe is the Gulliver of Lilliputian Weimar, always in doubt but always rescuing himself and perfecting his intellectual, artistic and moral development. For decades Goethe had been the philistine companion of writers and scholars who used him for their fashionable obscurantism. Mann now cleansed his portrait of reactionary filth. While the German bourgeoisie was degrading itself to the utmost, wading in the bloodstained swamp of a drunken barbarism, here was the image of its highest potentialities, of its, doubtless, problematic but also truthful and forward-pointing humanism.

It is only with the deepest reverence and love that one can

[1] *als Soldat und brav*: 'as a soldier and brave'. The quotation is from Goethe's *Faust*, part one. The words belong to the dying Valentin, Gretchen's brother, who perishes at Faust's hand in a duel to defend his sister's honour. The quotation is used as a chapter heading in *The Magic Mountain* where it ironically applies to the death of Castorp's military cousin, Joachim, whom illness has prevented from dying for his country.

treat this book. It saved Germany's honour in the hour of its most dreadful degradation. But this novel of Goethe is more than a monumental song of consolation for a drunken people hurling itself nihilistically into the abyss of fascism. It returns to the past in order to give promise for the future. By re-creating the best that German bourgeois culture had achieved, Mann seeks to awaken its buried, aberrant and brutalized potentialities. Mann's appeal rang with a primal moral optimism; what was possible once could always be realized again.

This is not a forced interpretation. At the end of his important essay *Goethe as Representative of the Bourgeois Age* Mann says: 'The burgher is lost, and loses track with the new or coming world, if he cannot bring himself to part from the life-destroying, easy-going ideologies that still condition him, and address himself stoutly to the future. The new, the social world, the organized, planned and unified world in which humanity will be freed from such human unneccesary burdens, injurious to self-respect and common sense; this world will come, and it will be the world of that great practical sense to which effective minds, all those opposed to a decadent and provincial soulfulness, must today subscribe. It will come, for an outward and rational order of things, adequate to the stage which human intelligence has now reached, must be created, or—in the worst case—be established by violent revolution, in order that the things of the soul may once more be justified. The great sons of the bourgeoisie, who grew out of that stage into the intellectual and super-bourgeois, are witnesses that boundless possibilities lie in the bourgeois stage, possibilities of unlimited self-release and self-conquest. The times challenge the middle class to remind itself of its native potentialities and to become equal to them both mentally and morally. The right to power is dependent upon the historic task to which one feels and may feel oneself called. If we deny it or are not adequate to it, we shall disappear; we shall simply yield the stage in favour of a human type free from the assumptions, the commitments and the outworn prejudice which—one sometimes fears—may prevent the bourgeoisie of Europe from being adequate to the task of guiding state and economy into a new world.'

The figure of Goethe then points out a new path for the German bourgeoisie, a path into the future. Even today Thomas Mann is still seeking the German bourgeois who has the will and the ability to take this path boldly. But Goethe is too distant a spiritual microcosm, separated from us by far too many crises, and on the other hand (especially in Mann's realization of him) far too remote a future ideal for the Professor Corneliuses or Hans Castorps of today to follow as their necessary next step forward, the step which will take the German bourgeois out of his abyss of humiliation, and relieve him of his deservedly tormented conscience and self-inflicted despair. There is an important connection missing here, although Mann is such a great artist of connections. It is missing because it is absent from the life of the German bourgeois, too. And Mann's artistic truthfulness never allows him to depict something which is not present in German bourgeois reality.

Typically, the German language, otherwise so rich, has not a word to express what we are speaking of now. The French speak of 'citoyen' as against 'bourgeois', the Russians of 'grazhdanin'. There is no word for it because German history has never produced the thing itself. Even in Mann's fine essay on Platen, the militant *citoyen* makes only a sporadic and peripheral appearance. In comparing Goethe and Schiller Mann says of Schiller that he 'manifests the French side of his nature'. Yet to say this of Schiller is another example of Mann's uncompromising veracity and his firm roots in the German national character. For probably no-one had ever shown such genuine sympathy with, or described so delicately, Schiller's heroic and self-consuming struggle for his art as Mann in his *Novelle A Weary Hour*. If, then, there is a blank here its cause is to be sought not in the limitations of Mann himself, but in the world whose mirror he was fated to be. Germany had suffered disastrously for it in the past and no doubt will do so again in the future, should it remain.

It would be quite unjust to suggest that Thomas Mann did not see this problem. Indeed, the whole point of his tireless and unavailing search was that (though for a long time unconsciously) he was really seeking a *German citoyen*, the German word, concept and essence of the *citoyen* who was also the true bourgeois. Hence his Faustian impatience with his every conclusion.

Settembrini is powerless before Naphta's social demagogy because he is only the epigone of a real *citoyen*. Robespierre and St. Just, Büchner and Heine never connected a genuinely free, fully consistent bourgeois democracy with the defence of the capitalist upper stratum and its often reactionary and antinational, selfish interests. Nor does Thomas Mann. His work, which began by condemning the Hagenströms, broadened out into Castorp's unease at the cruelty and inhumanity of life under capitalism. Both as creator and as critic, Mann saw to the heart of Settembrini's intellectual and political limitations. Indeed, as we have seen, he goes much further. He prescribed socialism as the future task of the bourgeois for whom he has been looking. If he has been unable, therefore, to create a *citoyen* spirit in his work which could stand against the fascist reaction, the fault was not his but lay in the post-1848 development of the German middle class. It is for this reason that, ever since his conversion to democracy, Thomas Mann has sought to link arms with the workers. This was not merely a tactical coalition; it was an alliance for the regeneration of German life and culture. This is what he writes: 'What would be needed, what would after all be typically German, would be an alliance, a compact between the conservative culture-idea and revolutionary social thought: to put it pointedly, as I have elsewhere done once before, an understanding between Greece and Moscow. It would be well with Germany, I repeat. She would have found herself, as soon as Karl Marx shall have read Friedrich

Hölderlin. Such a contact, moreover, is about to be established. But I must add that if it is onesided it will bear no fruit.'

This is indeed an impressive cultural programme for the German bourgeois. We do not consider it an accident that Hölderlin is chosen to represent German literature, for the point would be lost if one substituted the name of any other German poet, say Mörike, even though, in introducing his idea Mann links Hölderlin and Greece with the notion of a conservative culture. He overlooked the fact that the citizen of the Greek polis was the archetype of the *citoyen* and that Hölderlin was Germany's greatest *citoyen*-poet. Neither was remotely connected with any kind of German 'conservative culture-idea'. Nor is it important to know whether or not the real Marx in fact read Hölderlin (as far as I know he did). The important thing is how far the heroic, though sparse, traditions of real democracy in Germany were still alive and above all could come to life again in the German working class. Since Marx and Engels they had been buried under reactionary falsification. One mark of the poverty of German history common to both bourgeoisie and working class is the fact that Marx and Engels have so far not entered into the national cultural heritage as Lenin and Stalin have in Russia. The further development, the future, the rebirth of Germany depends to a great extent on how far German workers and bourgeois will succeed in mobilizing the reserves of freedom and progress in their history for their future national life. How far will this be able to replace the tradition which runs Goethe—Schopenhauer—Wagner—Nietzsche (which Mann himself used to accept and the last three members of which the Fascists have rightly claimed as their own) with a Lessing—Goethe—Hölderlin—Büchner—Heine—Marx tradition? Mann's portrait of Goethe gives a promising start to such a change.

And that is no accident. I have been able to say precious little about the specifically artistic sides of Mann's work. His rank I have taken for granted and have simply picked out one or two important incidents to illustrate certain critical stages in Germany's development. Let me take just one more such example. Thomas Mann's intimate relationship with all that is best in German literature should have emerged even from my very brief remarks. Yet even in the pure literary sense his role goes beyond this. It was Mann who first made Russian literature an essential part of German culture in the same way as Goethe gave us Shakespeare. In both cases it was a more than literary annexation, as is suggested by Thomas Mann in the important conversation on literature and life in *Tonio Kröger*. He points out that in Russia's 'holy literature' there is none of the hostile opposition between art and life which filled his own early work. Why not? The answer is clear. It is because Russian literature really has been the conscience of the Russian people and the voice of the *grazhdanin* spirit, from the Decembrist rising to the October revolution and from then on to the present day. The history of the great Russian realist literature from Pushkin to Gorki is interwoven—though never in a simple way—with the freedom struggles of the Russian people. And it is an instructive, though shameful, fact about Germany's ideological development that while its own classical philosophy ran to seed in its bourgeois homeland and turned to reaction, in Russia (and only in Russia) Hegel and Feuerbach found progressive thinkers to carry on their work.

Thomas Mann's aesthetic and ethical horizon took in both Goethe and Tolstoy. As a writer and a realist he has never been modern in the decadent sense. Hence he has been able to continue the best traditions of German literature. His form has never submitted to the disintegrating tendencies of decadence— rhetoric, declamation, decoration, brilliance, pseudo-scientific erudition, but has retained a genuine poetic totality.

Right through, from *Weltanschauung* to form, Mann's work is deeply progressive. His present achievement, and what we hope is to come, will contribute to the regeneration of the German spirit in a way which cannot be overestimated. Mann is still in search of his bourgeois today. For the German bourgeois has yet to be found. And he will not be found until he discovers within himself the *citoyen*, the *grazhdanin*. In this search Thomas Mann's role is crucial. His admirers are certain that his Faustian search for bourgeois man will never cease and that, like Faust, he will always give this answer to the devil of reaction:

> *Werd' ich beruhigt je mich auf ein Faulbett legen,*
> *So sei es gleich um mich getan!*
> *Kannst du mich schmeichelnd je belügen,*
> *Dass ich mir selbst gefallen mag,*
> *Kannst du mich mit Genuss betrügen:*
> *Das sei für mich der letzte Tag!*

> *Should ever a bed of ease content me,*
> *Then let me perish instantly!*
> *If you by flattery can bemuse me*
> *Into a self-complacency,*
> *Or with the sweets of life delude me:*
> *Let that day be the last for me!*

The Tragedy of Modern Art

I

THOMAS Mann's *Dr. Faustus* and the cycle of *Joseph* novels are a remarkable achievement to represent the mature work of a single writer. They form a monumental recapitulation and systematization of the subject-matter of his earlier period. What were previously études, capriccios and sonatous have become whole symphonies. This formal development, however, is not just a formal matter; it never is in the work of really significant artists. The symphonic complications and syntheses issue from a widening, deepening and generalizing of the content of Mann's original subject-matter. The growing formal complexity is dictated by the inner logic of his early themes. The characters, their relationships and experiences tended towards universality. If one looks at his early writing, one can see how little his development may be understood in formal terms. True, he starts off with a large novel which is pronouncedly universal in character, *Buddenbrooks*. In a certain sense it strikes all the notes of his later critique of capitalist society. And yet, compared even with later short stories, the first novel is much sparser, much less polyphonic.

It is along these lines that one should view Mann's development. The *Joseph* cycle and *Dr. Faustus* mark the culmination. They form a mature *oeuvre* of a very special type. They were specifically conditioned by the epoch in which they were conceived, that is by the culture of the imperialist period and its particular German variant.

47

Thomas Mann's general development runs interestingly parallel to Goethe's. At the same time it contrasts with his. Both writers had a flair for generalization, both lived through upheavals which changed the whole appearance of the world, and both grew towards real universality by struggling with the problems of this change. Growth of this kind is not something matter-of-course, even for writers of world-wide importance; it is, in fact, extremely rare. The 1848 crisis simply cast a shadow over the last works of Balzac. It affected Dickens similarly; and, while it may have deepened his later work and sharpened his social criticism, it never led him to draw the right conclusions. Then take Tolstoy. His work does not, as a result of increased social antagonism, suffer in the same way as Keller's does in *Martin Salander*; he never loses his monumental epic sense. But nor does he bring to culmination, universalize the ideas and subjects he broached in his youth. Yet this is what distinguishes Goethe and Mann. And clearly, if one can establish this typology in two outstanding writers, one is up against a deeper problem.

We would distort the problem if we simply took this abstract and general parallel and tried to apply it in its immediate form. For the basis, intellectual, moral, artistic, of such similarity of development is only one component of the parallel. It does not give us the *apriori* 'structure' of Goethe's and Mann's intellectual and artistic personality. This 'structure' underwent numerous and shattering changes before it assumed the universality of maturity. The essential changes were the great events of the day. Whatever we think of the innate and acquired personality—emotional, intellectual, artistic—of Goethe and Mann (and we hope that our studies have never denied a basis for such an estimate), this is only one component of the interaction with the great events of an age which changed mankind. It is this interaction which determines the divergences within the parallel or, if such a formula comes closer to reality, the convergence of certain decisive influences within the opposition.

In a letter to Count Reinhard, Goethe himself stated that,

during his maturity, he was wrestling all the time with the problems raised by the French Revolution. I think we must take this statement in a more general sense than its immediate formulation. Goethe's stormy youth was lived in the atmosphere which preceded the French Revolution. The outbreak of the Revolution and its results determined the Utopian hopes which Goethe had as a grown man for the renewal of society and of man within it. The social and human basis of his old age is the post-revolutionary development of Continental capitalism, which contrasts with the collapse of the last 'heroic period' of the bourgeoisie, the period of Napoleon's rule. He is resigned *vis-à-vis* the present, but for the future retains an optimistic vision. Goethe's style matches this intellectual and historical development by becoming increasingly abstract. His later works are more and more reflective. The burden of ideas puts an ever-increasing strain on the artistic form, which becomes increasingly stylized and artificial. The tension between criticism and Utopian hope, between resignation towards the present and optimism towards mankind grew constantly and became ever more difficult to bridge artistically. For this reason Goethe's old age is often wrongly said to be marked by a decline in creative powers.

Mann's development is in many ways parallel, but, essentially it goes in the opposite direction. His early work is determined by the stuffy atmosphere of 'power-protected inwardness' in imperialist Germany. The important experience of his maturity is the development of world crisis, which upsets his own youthful outlook; and then his break with that outlook. His old age was taken up with a ceaseless publicist struggle against fascism. Mann's development, therefore, while it has the same consistency as Goethe's, leads to quite the opposite results. Goethe becomes subject to an ever-increasing abstraction of style for the very reason that he becomes more historical in outlook. Mann, for whom imperialist war and fascism take the place of the French Revolution and Napoleon, becomes more concrete, enriches his artistic picture. In particular, he fills in the social and historical determinants of his characters.

It is thus the moments of destiny in bourgeois society which determine the creative path of Germany's greatest bourgeois writers. Goethe's *Faust* ends with the scenes in Heaven, which are tangible because they spring from Utopian hope in a renewal and liberation of man based on economic foundations and a social morality. Mann's *Faustus* is tragic in atmosphere precisely because these foundations have been undermined and shattered. The same similarity, which works itself out as an antithesis in their art, conditions the peculiar relationship of both to contemporary literary trends. It is characteristic of both Goethe and Mann that, though they never ignore new literary trends, they greet them with reserve. Both are concerned with the totality of human relationships and the progress of mankind, though they consider progress a very contradictory phenomenon. This is their basic attitude. It allows them to develop a fine sense for the actual changes in men, for the relationships and influences which manifest themselves in artistic innovation, and to determine whether such innovation is justified. It makes them critical of all tendencies which canonise superficial or indeed reactionary currents in the real social and historic world. This is clearly to be seen in Goethe's dealings with Romanticism. Mann, too, much as he welcomed very many forms of modernism, spoke of himself as an opponent of 'anti-intellectual movements'. As he clearly saw, 'the fashion for the "irrational" frequently marks a knavish desire to throw overboard all the achievements and principles which have not merely made the European a European but have turned men into human beings.' We will discuss the stylistic consequences of this attitude later.

In this parallel we have laid so much weight on the contrasts —between stylistic problems and the epochs which conditioned them—that one may well wonder how just a parallel it is. It is based first on Goethe's decisive role in Mann's development. But it goes deeper. Mann is helped in raising his early problems to a universal level by the universality of *Wilhelm Meister* and *Faust*. And this again is not a formal influence. Even if we understand form in the widest possible sense there is nothing in common between the *Joseph* and the *Wilhelm Meister* novels. The same applies to the *Faustus* novel. Despite the similarities in the problem and certain individual incidents it bears no resemblance to Goethe's poem. The parallel is rather one of inner development which, translated into form, appears as an antithesis, because of the social and historical differences we have just mentioned.

What then does this parallel consist in? Let us take the *Joseph* cycle first. Both writers treat their early problems in a very subjective manner; the tone is lyrical and only one or two themes predominate. In keeping with their general outlook they state their problems more or less 'timelessly', that is in supra-historical, in purely psychological and moral terms. Form is self-contained. Later on the same problems acquire historical concreteness, they are socially generalized. They appear more symphonic and polyphonic. Of course, there are important enough differences even at the outset. *Werther* is much more consciously social in idea than *Tonio Kröger*. Nevertheless, the parallel lines are sufficiently clear, running in the one case from *Werther* to *Wilhelm Meister*, in the other from *Tonio Kröger* to the *Joseph* cycle.

I think it was Slochower who first pointed out that Joseph was a continuation of Kröger. There is no room here to go into this deeply. Suffice it that Joseph resumes the spiritual and moral problem of Tonio Kröger (and his brethren in Mann's world), but with no direct reference to the artist and his life. Or to put it better: *Tonio Kröger* is simply concerned with the opposition between art and life. The same concern appears in the *Joseph* novels in two ways, first as a particular kind of attitude to life which, given the right subjective and objective conditions, may produce art; secondly, if taken in a general human sense and related to social conditions, as a central problem of bourgeois society. Goethe shows this same line of development,

51

as we can see if we compare *Wilhelm Meister* with *Werther*, *Tasso* ('Weither intensified'[1]) and the early 'theatrical mission' version of *Wilhelm Meister*. One can find many parallels in the transitions, too. For instance, one could without exaggeration call Aschenbach in *Death in Venice* an 'intensified' Tonio Kröger.

But the very plenitude of parallels reveals the difference. Let us take the main question, the relationship of art to life. Art for Goethe is a means of mastering reality and hence plays a part in the development of an all-round, harmonious man. This question sprang from the great problems of his day, before and after the French Revolution; it sprang from the development of capitalism. Goethe's essential aim was to preserve humanism and adapt it to these historical conditions; hence the relationship between art and life had certain specific meanings for him.

We can only indicate them under headings here. What he was mainly concerned with was human and moral self-mastery as against capitalist bureaucratic one-sidedness, as against dilettant-ism and dissipation of energy. This is how he put it in his well-known letter to Herder which he wrote as a young man on reading Pindar: 'If you can stand boldly in a chariot with four fresh horses rearing up spiritedly in the reins, and can direct their forces—whipping in the one that gets out of line and bringing down the one that rears up, giving rein, guiding, turn-ing, whipping, stopping and starting again, until all sixteen hooves are moving in rhythm towards the finishing post—you have achieved mastery.' This is the key to Werther's desire for socially useful employment (of which Napoleon disapproved). This explains, too, the relationship between Tasso and Antonio; it also explains Wilhelm Meister's development: the danger of wasting one's substance in artistic onesidedness. But Goethe also experienced the first symptoms of the isolation of art in bour-geois society. He fought a double battle against this tendency, though he came to feel more and more certain of its ineluct-

[1]Goethe's description of his play *Torquato Tasso*.

ability. On the one hand art as such, the purity of art must be saved from the anti-aesthetic forces of the day. On the other the social character of art must be preserved in face of the threatening isolation. This is why Goethe constantly and ever-increasingly strove for a 'great world' (which did not exist in his Germany).

This is the aim of the Utopias in the two *Wilhelm Meister* novels.

By Thomas Mann's time this process was complete. In capitalist society the isolation of the modern artist and of modern art was an accomplished fact. Especially in Germany, for there the events of 1848 and 1871 had narrowed down to an extreme degree the scope for any kind of dynamic interaction between art and social life (it was still possible in France, for example). Hence the young Thomas Mann can see no way out; the 'world' is excluded from the atmosphere of his art. In the First World War he makes his desperate effort to attach himself to a German communal tradition, to find a philosophic explanation and justification for the opposition between Germany and the democratic West. (For instance, the distinctions between culture and civilization, between writer and *littérateur* in his wartime writings.) Yet in all this the dialectic of his creative work is evident. It comes out especially in his exposure of the human contradictions of Prussianism; in this way *Death in Venice* is an anticipatory criticism of the war writings. Then there is the quite justified criticism of Western bourgeois-democratic civilization. Once these contradictions could be seen in their totality the main threat to human values in the epoch of imperialism could be spotlighted. But this was to come later.

I have analysed this development in *In Search of Bourgeois Man*. Here let me simply note the new themes in Mann's writing. The opposition between life and death is the determining factor in his early work, too. But there, before the crisis of the First World War, it forms a monochrome composition. Life appears simply as a horizon, the object of hopeless yearning. The real content is the outward and inward victory of death.

The crisis in Mann's outlook renders his problems more specific. The death principle becomes sickness, decay, the abyss, and sympathy with sickness or decay. For the isolated individual in bourgeois society life (the world) is still unattainable. Even the younger Mann had seen that health and life must unite in a community, but he was unable to give any concrete shape to this unity. It polarized into Hans Hansen on the one hand and Klöterjahn on the other. Again the adherents of death in the early works are often caricatured; Mann approaches them polemically (Tristan, Bajazzo). This tendency now turns into self-irony (Professor Cornelius); into the philistine phantasy of *The Magic Mountain*; and culminates in the (fascist) hypnosis of the sorcerer and the bewitched (*Mario and the Magician*). We cannot analyse this development here. These few remarks are simply to show that the educational novel emerges as an organic climax to Thomas Mann's development. The road Joseph travels leads from isolation to human and social community. But earlier, too, and (not by accident) speaking of Goethe, Mann had defined the idea of education as 'a bridge and crossing-place from the inner, personal world of man to the social world'. It is the road from pure contemplation of self—which in young Joseph and Mann's other early heroes reaches narcissism—to social activity. This is the way in which health and life must overcome corruption, sickness and death.

The arena of the new educational novel is biblical Egypt, which relieves Mann from having to deal directly with contemporary society. This has a special importance for the educational novel because, as we have shown elsewhere, Mann as a writer is firmly anti-Utopian, in striking contrast to the Utopian ending of *Wilhelm Meister's Apprenticeship* and to the whole conception of *Wilhelm Meister's Wanderings*. Nevertheless, a historical subject (and a Utopia, too) in the hands of a genuine writer must express the essential lineaments of the present. Here is the land of death. Mann sketches in the crisis of faith which has struck Egyptian society, presenting it with gentle and affectionate irony as the background and impetus of Joseph's education. In this country of death we see, on the one hand, the decadence which denies life—in Petepre and the young Pharaoh; its accents are diverse. We also see goodness, intelligence, humanity and justice, but always in the most varied forms of impotence. On the other hand corruption stalks undisguised: in the palace Macchiavellianism and obscurantist fanaticism of the High Priest Bechnekes; in the barbaric passions of Petepre's wife, which are normally hidden behind the polished surface of this realm of the dead. From a purely personal standpoint, Eni's fate is very moving, but at the same time it provides an individual, human image of the growth of fascism. Both extremes appear in grotesque form in the contrasting pair of dwarfs.

This is the world in which Joseph is educated. His education had started of course, in the bosom of his family, in Palestine. Mann's description in both cases catches the present. It swings to and fro with delightful wit and irony between the 'once-upon-a-time', the 'never-and-ever' of legend and a deeply humane orientation on the present. If this orientation is not there, why recount the legend in such detail? And Thomas Mann, though again with irony and reservation, places the personality and style of the narrator right in the foreground. This orientation appears in the inner identity of Tonio Kröger and Joseph. But the theme now is much more humanely stated. It is consciously posed within a wide historical frame.

It starts off with a gifted, self-satisfied and self-absorbed youth who lives in a dream-world and imagines that others love him more than they love themselves. This provokes a clash—and the first 'pit' of the novel. In the pit Joseph undergoes a decisive change, although he retains the belief in his own irresistible charm. This accounts for his guilt when he comes into conflict with Eni's passion: the second pit. In each case he is saved from complete ruin only by the generosity of others, in the first case Ruben, in the second Petepre. Here, although outwardly there is not the slightest reference to the present, Thomas Mann has in fact revealed a deep trait of the German psyche and the German hubris. For it is just this belief in its own irresistible power that is one of the important spiritual and moral reasons for Germany's downfall.

What Joseph's education teaches him is how to overcome this attitude. The decisive factor, however, is not outer-directed activity as such. Activity of this kind was possible in Petepre's house, yet it did not prevent him from repeating his fall. It did not change the structure of his type, the belief that his own vision, his own representation of the world must be superior to objective reality. Only after his second fall, and in close connection with the religious revolution of the youthful Pharaoh, does his real change of heart take place. His first fall was linked with religion and social reaction. Now Joseph becomes the leader into life of the realm of the dead. From the clever manager of one household he turns into the Provider, the revolutionary and dictatorial leader of a whole people. At this point, where it seems there could be no room at all for German allusions, the novel in fact is only too German.

Thomas Mann on many occasions called Schiller a 'French' type in contrast to the German Goethe. As always, even where he goes wrong, Mann puts his finger on a real and important problem. In identifying democracy and politics in the modern world, Mann intends that democracy is impossible without real politics. It is unimportant that he puts this negativity unpolitically, indeed anti-politically (hence his false treatment of the 'unpolitical Goethe'). Nor does it matter that he exaggerates: he is making a very general and therefore abstract statement. The main thing is that he is proposing an attitude which is objectively important and will have a decisive bearing on his later work. Its full implication will become clear when I analyse *Dr. Faustus*.

Goethe is not unpolitical but represents a typically German kind of politics, a politics which ignores the idea of an active world 'below'. He first expresses this tendency as an enlightener, then in his appreciation of technical and economic changes as autonomous factors of development. 'I am not worried,' he said to Eckermann, 'that Germany may never be united. Our good highroads and future railways will look after the rest.' Hence his attitude to the Suez, the Panama and the Rhine-Danube Canals. Hence many important elements in the conclusion to *Faust*.

Schiller, like most German bourgeois democrats, thought that it was impossible to find a model, a concrete embodiment, of democratic, not to mention revolutionary, action on German soil. Thus in Schiller we find the typical literary expression of Germany's distorted development: the model of revolution from above. It is no accident that the great scene between Posa and Philipp, which puts this attitude at its most poetic, will always sweep a German audience off its feet.[1] This conception runs through German history. It is true, for instance, not only of Lassalle's *Sickingen*,[2] but also of the politically radical, the 'French' Heinrich Mann's *Henri IV*.

It is no accident then, no betrayal of his German heritage, if we find Thomas Mann taking the path of *Don Carlos*. But does it mean that he is following Schiller's representation of German reality? For one thing the intervening century and a half had brought about a qualitative change in the situation. What in Schiller was simply a reflection of German backwardness, of Germany's objective and subjective unreadiness for democratic change now acquires a new accent, namely a lack of faith in mass activity, a disbelief in the creative powers which come from 'below'.

Mann's development leads beyond democracy to an acknowledgment of the inevitability of socialism. Yet this possibility does not enter into his creative work. The reasons could be

[1] The reference is to Schiller's *Don Carlos*.
[2] Ferdinand Lassalle (1825-1864), the German Socialist, was also an imaginative writer. Sickingen is the knight who led the peasants during the great German peasant revolt at the time of the Reformation.

personal, but their roots go deeper. I have often explained that the great strength of Mann's realism is that he only deals with what actually exists in German reality. He excludes what is merely desirable. What is real he will follow to the roots, but he will never anticipate the future. This is his strength as a realist.

At the same time it somewhat narrows his social and historical horizon. For, firstly, although all movements from below in Germany have so far failed, this says nothing of their future. Secondly, these failures—with all their causes—form an organic part of the physiognomy of the German people. Mann shows some of the social and psychological causes and many of the results of this situation. But the phenomenon itself is missing from his picture of the world. For this reason the whole world 'below' plays a very much smaller role in his writing than it does in real life. And this makes his democracy, his socialism and his struggle against contemporary reaction sometimes abstract, vacillating or indeed directionless. One might object that none of these matters has anything to do with the story of Joseph. To that one must reply that a writer's theme—particularly in the case of Mann whose work is so organic—is never a thing of chance. The fact that Mann handles the myth with such affection and such restrained irony means that it responds to his innermost purposes. It is impossible to reconstruct the original vision of a great writer from his work. Nevertheless, it does seem that the realm of the dead, the figure of Joseph and his development as well as certain other protagonists belong to the primal source of the work. But so then must the revolution from above which is already present in outline in the legend, thereby acquiring a matter-of-course and more-than-ordinary validity. All that I have said constitutes (quite consciously) a criticism from outside. But this outsideness is what Mann's telling of his myth requires. It forms the premise of the elaborate narrative which constantly returns to the present from its deeply-charted courses into history-cum-myth. The narrator lives at all times in the present, and Mann, with his gentle irony, ceaselessly reminds us of this fact. There is never any direct reference to the present, there is no allegory or symbolism. The realm of the dead no more 'signifies' Germany than Cipolla did Mussolini. But the work as a concrete whole relates to the concrete whole of our own day, though the relationship is complicated and checked throughout with irony. If a story suggests no *tua res agitur* which can apply to the present, then it fails as a story, its plot loses credence.

So, too, with the revolution from above. Here again we see an important affinity with Goethe, though yet still more important divergences. The dialectic of education takes them both from the 'small world' of mere personal living into the 'great world' of social life. For both (for the reasons just given) this 'great world' is a world 'above'. 'Above' means work *for* all; it is never an achievement or act *of* the masses. Therefore it never interacts with them, has no inner relationship with them. Joseph the 'provider' remains just as isolated after the success of his revolution from above, as the Marquis Posa who so tragically failed. Whatever the social content of Joseph's education, it is only psychologically and morally an education in the social. Hence while Goethe does at least make his Utopian plea for a real 'great world', namely in the Utopian vision of a free people at the end of *Faust*, this real 'great world' disappears in Mann. What is essentially right about his thesis that politics and democracy are the same applies here. For it follows that a true 'great world' must be democratic. Thus while from a purely aesthetic point of view the revolution from above is the only possible conclusion, since it is based on the actual Joseph legend, this configuration has important consequences. Joseph's change of heart, his education, is the becoming-social of his psychology, moral outlook and behaviour. The resulting activity and effects of this education are brilliantly described. But no real 'great world' in fact emerges as it does in *Wilhelm Meister* and *Faust*, where the concluding vision reacts back on the whole work.

Mann's 'small world' simply acquires new psychological and moral dimensions, important as these are.

II

This relationship of the 'small' to the 'great world' forms the crux of *Dr. Faustus*. Some may doubt the absence of a 'great world' in the Joseph novels and argue that the social activity of the legendary Joseph and Pharaoh did in fact constitute *their* 'great world' and that I was simply reversing things by bringing in the present as a yardstick. But to do so was inevitable, even from an artistic standpoint. For whether or not a 'great world' is possible in the present plays a determining part in a writer's work. In Lassalle's *Sickingen* the Posa role, the revolution from above, was far more of an anachronism than in Schiller himself.

Looking at Mann's *Faustus*, then, we note that post-1848 Germany did not in fact produce any native, democratic 'great world', so that its absence is historically, and therefore artistically, authentic. On the other hand this image omits all the attempts of the working class to create a democratic 'great world' in Germany (though they come to nothing). Thomas Mann, therefore gives a picture of Germany up to 1945, which consists of the results but not the actual process. He writes an epilogue to Germany's cultural development and to her political and social mis-development. This epilogue is a prologue insofar as such a radical reckoning with the past, as occurs in this novel, inevitably, by the sheer force of self-criticism, contains elements of the future. The vision of a free people which Goethe's *Faust* elicits from the 'great world' was certainly Utopian in its day. Yet it had a real basis in history, for the whole of German classical literature and philosophy from Lessing to Heine was an ideological preparation for the democratic revolution of 1848. Thomas Mann's *Dr. Faustus*, however, forms the conclusion, the epilogue to the whole development after 1848.

For these reasons the new Faust is a Faust of the study. Nor does he seriously desire to leave it, that is to translate his aims into deeds. Into this study crowds the whole complex of Faust problems, for the link that binds a quest for truth and life with social practice has been severed from the outset. Here we have a Faust whose environment consists solely of the 'small world', the study as it interacts with whatever of life may and must come knocking at its door.

A Faust, then, in a Raabe atmosphere. This, of course, is not meant in the narrow literary sense, not even in the way one quite rightly talks of a Storm atmosphere in *Tonio Kröger*. It is a question rather of the basic problem of what is portrayed. With Raabe German literature, penned in by social and historical circumstances, stoically retires from the 'great world'. In Raabe's own works we see partly this forced retreat as such— the peripheral heroes who had once fought in the Wars of Liberation, in the *Burschenchaft* movement under Bolivar, etc., vainly seeking in these struggles a breakthrough to the 'great world', and partly, in the mass of his characters, the human deformation resulting from the lack of such attempts in contemporary Germany. Raabe's humour reveals with a tragicomic resignation the distortions which must occur in all men, in all Germans who suffer from the social constriction of their world. A hypertrophy of intellectual and emotional inwardness will often turn into boredom, desolation and grotesque or banal forms of philistinism.

This is what I mean by a Raabe atmosphere. The Faustus world of Thomas Mann differs from it not only by its incomparably higher artistic level, but also by the absence of any attempt, even a fruitless one, at a breakthrough to life. (I would mention the beautifully written Marie Godeau episode, where Mann brings out this deepest desire to fail with wonderful vividness.) Of course, the atmosphere of 'power-protected inwardness' that belongs to the Wilhelmine period turns ever more menacingly, with the social development of German imperialism and the defeat of the First World War, into a stifling prelude to barbarism. 'Power-protected inwardness' changes more and more definitely into the intellectual preparation, the cultural build-up of a new inhuman and anti-human reaction. Sometimes this occurs in good faith, sometimes in a vein of frivolity. But if the German spirit becomes social in this way, is 'politicized', (that is, if a more and more conscious anti-humanism can still be called 'spirit'), it does so in a (however changed) Raabe-like atmosphere. The 'small world' is confronted by no 'great' one; it reduces the themes and dimensions of the 'great world' to its own eccentric, esoteric, reactionary and increasingly barbaric philistinism.

It is in such a 'small world' that Mann's Faustus tragedy takes place. And it can be a real tragedy, despite its deliberately tragicomic features, because the study of the new Faust is made inaccessibly fast from the outside world; at least psychologically and morally. The intelligentsia with whom Mann's Faust, Adrian Leverkühn, comes into contact is rushing headlong into Fascist barbarism, performing a grotesque, snobbish death dance as it does so. He on the other hand lives a life of asceticism and otherworldly disdain. 'Unworldly' (*weltscheu*) most typically describes his response to the humanity of his day. But what is tragi-comic or, better, grotesquely tragic about his story is that, despite his self-imposed seclusion, the very themes he chooses for his work are most intimately related to the snobbish and reactionary tendencies of his time, if only in an ultimate sense. Next, his 'unworldliness', his monk-like repudiation of the affairs of men in his day and age opens the very door to the devil in his work and life.

Thus the study has a completely different meaning for the new Faust from that which it had for the old. Starting with the vain (magic) attempts at breakthrough, the study of the old Faust led into the 'great world'—the translation of ideas into social practice. This was the breakthrough. The study of the new Faust, on the other hand, is hermetically sealed from the outside social world. Yet only apparently so, for in reality it is the witches' kitchen where all the disaster-bearing tendencies of the times are brewed to their essence. This essence, this concentration may baffle and offend the outside world because it is so hard, uncompromising, so tragically unrelenting. Yet the unity between the two remains. The ideas, the problems, the form of Adrian Leverkühn's work are a *summa*, an encyclopaedia of what the spirit of this age is capable of bringing forth, both for good and for bad. Whatever is possessed in the way of 'world' by the German mind, in its 'power-protected inwardness', its socially conditioned 'drivenness', 'throwness-upon-itself' (to talk now existentially as the subject demands), this is contained quintessentially in the 'small world' of the study. Thus a modern *Faust* in a Raabe atmosphere modified by imperialism.

But this configuration of mental outlook and art is an international phenomenon of the entire imperialist period. In Germany it appears in its purest form, therefore at its most problematic and devilish. Thus only in his immediate person is Adrian Leverkühn a specifically German type. His universality extends far beyond Germany's geographical and intellectual frontiers. Just as Nietzsche and Spengler, Freud and Heidegger, despite their immediate German characteristics, are international phenomena, indeed from an international standpoint the veriest signposts of the intellectual disasters of the imperialist period, so, too, is the imagined music of Adrian Leverkühn.

The objective disappearance of the 'great world' is a general feature of the culture of the ruling classes in imperialism. The basic tendencies of the economics, politics and culture of imperialism (even in a bourgeois democracy) are deeply undemocratic and anti-democratic. The democracy which was won by revolution turns into a caricature of itself as the power of monopoly capital and the finance oligarchy increases and grows more reactionary. Its outward forms, its ideologies of 'freedom', become more hypocritical, contrasting ever more sharply with social reality, provoking ever louder opposition from thinking intellectuals. True this resistance has seldom struck at the real social substance of the new situation in which democracy finds itself under imperialism. Its most common form is opposition to democracy as such, treating it as a decadent social phenomenon, or questioning the possibility of any kind of democracy. This social and ideological situation lends the German version, including the intellectual and artistic form it takes, an international validity. In its debased German condition the disappearing 'great world' of democracy appears at once as a terrible and a tempting image, a symbol (however grotesquely twisted) of what is in store for bourgeois democracy, for the political and social fate of its culture.

This is not the place to examine the complicated inter-relationship between German and international anti-democracy, to pick out the common and distinguishing features in either the absence or disappearance of a 'great world'. We must limit ourselves to one or two remarks. The main thing is that the German relationship between the study of the new Faust and the objective and subjective impossibility of breaking out of it into the 'great world' determines the basic differences between Goethe's Mephistopheles and the embodiments of the devil in Mann's novel.

For the tempter appears here in two shapes. In comparison to the Reformation Goethe's devilish principle is spiritualized in the extreme. Yet the seductive offer of the kingdoms of the world and the glory of them remains. (I have explained in separate studies the very complicated relationship between Faust and Mephistopheles.) In Thomas Mann the question resolves itself into a caricature. The very earthly, ironic devil is the impresario Saul Fitelberg, a capitalist speculator in avant-garde music, whose stock-in-trade is 'the scandalous today which tomorrow will be the fashion, the dernier cri, the best-seller—in short, art'. He offers his services to Adrian Leverkühn: 'And still, figurez-vous, I have come to tempt you away, to betray you to a temporary unfaithfulness, to bear you on my mantle through the air and show you the kingdoms of the earth and the glory of them, to lay them at your feet . . .' He is rejected with utter contempt. Adrian Leverkühn wants, subjectively, nothing to do with the real social basis of his art. Yet, be it in terms of disdain, opposition, parody filled with pathos and irony, his art is ultimately an offspring of this basis and its culture, determined by them in content and form. He lives and works in the sincere illusion that he is independent of his social surroundings and of the social currents of his day, that he concedes nothing, yields nothing to them.

And this is true, at least on the surface. But if one looks more closely the picture is almost the opposite. Adrian Leverkühn knows quite well what the real historical situation of music (art or intellectual life in general) is in his day. Not only does he know this, but gives it his constant and energetic thought. Every stylistic problem springs from this preoccupation. The time, the present is at every point unconducive to art, to music —how then is it possible to create music of a really high artistic order without breaking free of one's time, without firmly and actively renouncing it.

Even the young Leverkühn was aware of this question when choosing his career and changing over from theology to music. True, at first it is only a personal problem. He says he is 'unworldly', talks of his inner coldness, of the boredom which very soon attacks him whatever may capture his interest. He lacks that 'robust naïveté' which he knows is essential to an artist.

But this coldness is not simply a psychological quality of Adrian. It represents a value for him. He may long for warmth but, inwardly, he regards a coldly critical, bored attitude as superior, as more in keeping with the real nature of the world. It is typical that even in early youth he should talk ironically about the 'cow warmth' of normal music. These are all still the general traits of a modern artist in Mann's characterization; in this respect Leverkühn is merely a younger brother of Tonio Kröger and Gustav von Aschenbach.

More important is the fact that the general and at the same time specific problem of modern art arises as soon as he chooses his career, even though initially in the form of a personal difficulty. In a long and important letter to his first teacher he speaks of his 'abandoned' habit of finding something funny in the most serious and moving musical passages: 'I may have tears in my eyes at the same time, but the desire to laugh is irresistible—I have always had to laugh, most damnably, at the most mysterious and impressive phenomena. I fled from this exaggerated sense of the comic into theology, in the hope that it would give relief to the tickling—only to find there too a perfect legion of ludicrous absurdities.'

So far this is still just a personal attitude of Adrian's, a heightened version of the Kröger-Aschenbach response, although the heightening has already turned it into something qualitatively new. The difference comes out as Adrian continues his reflections. He goes on to discuss the musical problems which arise from his attitude: 'Why does almost everything seem to me like its own parody? Why must I think that almost all, no, all the methods and conventions of art today are good for parody only?' He is now objectifying his attitude, canonizing it as the only viable artistic approach *today*. Adrian's teacher, who is an artistic fanatic, fortifies him. He replies to his pupil's confession, underlining all the social, historical and artistic reasons that justify such an attitude. He writes: 'Art needed just his sort today ... the coolness, the "quickly-satisfied intelligence", the eye for the stale and absurd, the early fatigue, the capacity for disgust—all that was perfectly calculated to make a profession of the talent bound up with it. Why? Because it belonged only in part to the private personality; for the rest it was of an extra-individual nature, the expression of a collective feeling for the historical exhaustion and vitiation of the means and appliances of art, the boredom with them and the search for new ways.'

It is impossible here to follow the further emergence of these subjective and objective determinants of modern art in Adrian

Leverkühn's musical development. Thomas Mann's achievement in showing the genesis, structure and impact of his works forms an isolated summit in the world's literature. Hitherto the tragedy of the artist has, almost without exception, been presented from the standpoint of the relationship and conflict between the artist and life, between art and reality. This is largely true of the early Mann. Here, however, the work of art itself is called into question. Therefore, its genesis and structure must be shown; the tragic predicament of modern art must be demonstrated by the work itself.

Only Balzac has ever attempted anything of this sort—in his *Chef d'oeuvre Inconnu* and *Gambara*. But these are no more than *novella*-like episodes within the whole of the *Comédie Humaine* (although they prophetically foreshadow many of the predicaments of modern art). Mann goes further than Balzac in two ways. Balzac was aware of some important difficulties facing the modern artist in the choice of his means of expression, and with great power and insight showed the basic failure of such a choice to render the reality aimed at. Yet this was but a brilliant anticipation of a future tendency. Hence in the *Comédie Humaine* as a whole it could be no more than an episode. Further the conflict he presented was tragic in a purely objective sense. His hero, Frenhofer, is seen psychologically and morally as an artist of the old school, confident and unproblematic. The insoluble conflict arises simply out of the dialectical contradiction between modern means of expression and the aesthetic necessities of an obdurately tangible subject.

Following Balzac we have the long series of artist tragedies in which the personal and moral relationship of the modern artist to life becomes problematic. Mann's early works form the conclusion to this development. At this point, as we have just shown, the modern artist's attitude enters into the structure of his work. Mann's great feat in this novel is to have portrayed this process with such a wealth, depth and palpability, that we can see Leverkühn's whole problematic, creative process, the objective predicament of his works vividly before us. Indeed the content of the whole, great novel is essentially the growth and meaning of these works. And Thomas Mann has succeeded not only in creating a whole series of such works and in letting the reader feel that each is an individual spiritual and artistic entity. He has also made his hero a lively and differentiated personality despite the fact that he is solely a composer, solely an artist who has practically no life outside his art.

Briefly *apropos* of Adrian Leverkühn's music: it is, of course, as much Mann's original creation as the ideas of the ageing Faust are those of Goethe. Just as it would have been absurd to have made prior claims on behalf of Giordano Bruno and Spinoza, so today Schönberg only makes a fool of himself to insist that Leverkühn's music is his 'intellectual property'. For the originality of the *Faustus* music is not its atonality as such, but the general character of contemporary music as the concentrated expression of intellectual and moral decadence. It is this which causes the tragic cleavage in Adrian Leverkühn; his tragic end expresses the logical conclusion, the insolubility of these tendencies. But composers who are content to paddle in decadence, yet would not dream of pursuing its tendencies to a tragic consequence will have nothing to do with (and quite rightly) the tragic issue of Leverkühn's art and personality. They automatically exclude themselves from the spiritual world of Mann's novel. For the stature of this work is determined by its tragic outcome. It is this which raises Adrian Leverkühn's lonely person above the chattering chorus of modern decadence, yet makes him representative of it.

In other essays I have often shown how the 'intellectual physiognomy' of characters in modern fiction is fast disappearing. The heroes of literature are sinking to deeper intellectual lows. Thomas Mann has always been one of the few exceptions in this time of decadence to have set themselves against the current of bourgeois art, against the transformation of literature and art into a gallery of refined still-lifes. Here he has created a work, certainly in conscious opposition to the anti-intellectualism of modern literature and art, in which one might say that the highly differentiated and rounded characters have sprung pure from the mind. This is the first thing to establish—the unique achievement in the world's literature today. To analyse it properly would require a separate study.

We have set ourselves a different problem. We wish to treat the novel as a *Zeitroman*, a novel of the times, as the tragic quintessence of bourgeois culture of the present. For this reason we cannot go into the wonderful detail, but must return to the basic problem. What Mann does here is to give an analysis of the predicament which besets the whole of modern art. He reveals on the one hand how the purely subjective, that which is estranged from and despises all community is rooted in the modern bourgeois individualism of the imperialist epoch; and on the other how this dissolves, just as inevitably, every bond, old and new, both with society and within a work itself. For this reason Leverkühn's parodistic attitude is a mark of his intellectual honesty. Further, Mann shows how the same situation creates a longing for syntheses, for control, for order and organization, though such a longing has no real foundation in popular life, in the social world, but is the product of the same subjectivity which creates the disintegration. The longing for order, therefore, is itself indirectly a disintegrating tendency; hence it destroys itself.

In one passage Adrian's boyhood friend and biographer calls him an 'archaic-revolutionary schoolmaster'. Adrian himself talks of the self-destructive freedom in modern life and art. He says of this desire for synthesis: 'However, it could mean something necessary to the time, something promising a remedy in an age of destroyed conventions and the relaxing of all objective obligations—in short, of a freedom that begins to lie like a mildew upon talent and to betray traces of sterility'. The desire for synthesis, therefore, turns in a circle; it is the subjective expression of the *curculus vitiosus* of modern bourgeois art and culture. On the one hand it is the extreme of subjectivism, as much the product of the subject as is the freedom which destroys itself. On the other it expresses the wish for order at all costs and the readiness to submit to any such order, so long as it puts an end, with whatever means, to an arbitrary and aimless freedom.

At one point in Adrian's youth his teacher reads a paper about a member of an American sect, an amusing, odd, un-tutored man, who for the practical uses of his sect devised some crazy and quite arbitrary new musical 'theory of order'. Adrian naturally finds the theory very funny. But when his friend ridi-cules the inventor, he retorts: 'Leave me in peace with my old codger, I can do with him. At least he had a sense of order, and even a silly order is better than none at all.' Inevitably, then, this desire for order and synthesis, which springs from the modern disintegration of individuality and so remains purely subjective, continually verges on those tendencies which feed into imperialist reaction and ultimately fascism. What comes out here is the essential bond between the formal synthesis of modern art and the reactionary ideologies of the age.

Behind Leverkühn's music, therefore, lurks the deepest despair, the despair of a real artist for the social function of art, and not only art but bourgeois society itself in our time. He may attempt to break free from his position (though all such attempts will be purely in terms of his art). But he will only exacerbate these inner contradictions and hasten on the destruction of his art, whose premise is its divorce from life. Such attempts must lead objectively to the death of art. In a tragic moment the hero's lifelong friend and biographer, who still has the old, humanist devotion to art, writes: 'Far be it for me to deny the seriousness of art; but when it becomes serious then one rejects art and is not capable of it.' Lest it be said that this is a 'universal human' attitude, let us compare once again the times in which Goethe and Thomas Mann wrote. Goethe can still say of such crises and the function of art within them:

Und wenn der Mensch in seiner Qual verstummt,
Gab mir ein Gott, zu sagen, wie ich leide.

And if man's agony makes him dumb
A god gave me voice to say how I suffer.

Hence the suspicion which dawns on Leverkühn's friend and biographer, as he describes one of Leverkühn's most significant compositions, his *Apocalypse*, 'how near aestheticism and barbarism are to each other: aestheticism as the herald to barbarism. . . .' Hence he says of the work: 'How often has this intimidating work, in its urge to reveal in the language of music the most hidden things, the beast in man as well as his sublimest stirrings, incurred the reproach of blood-boltered barbarism and of bloodless intellectuality. I say incurred; for its idea, in a way, is to take in the life-history of music, from its pre-musical magic rhythmical elementary stage to its most complex consummation; and thus it does perhaps expose itself to such reproaches, not only in part but as a whole.' Continuing his analysis of the work he establishes (quite unconsciously) the connection between Leverkühn's music and the most deep-seated tendencies of dehumanization in the art of the imperialist period: 'The chorus is "instrumentalized", the orchestra "vocalized", to that degree and to that end that the boundary between man and thing seems shifted.' For this reason he sees the essential characteristic of the work as a conscious inversion of the functions of harmony and dissonance: 'The whole work is dominated by the paradox (if it is a paradox) that in it dissonance stands for the expression of everything lofty, solemn, pious, everything of the spirit; while consonance and firm tonality are reserved for the world of hell, in this context a world of banality and commonplace.'

By a remarkable coincidence (if coincidence it be) I had just finished reading *Dr. Faustus* when the Central Committee of the Communist Party of the Soviet Union published its decree on modern music. In Thomas Mann's novel this decree finds its fullest intellectual and artistic confirmation, particularly in those parts which so brilliantly describe modern music as such. For *Dr. Faustus* encompasses the whole of modern art, its problems of style (down to their most technical) and its human and social foundations.

These very sketchy remarks were necessary so that we should appreciate the full extent of the difference between the devils in Goethe and Mann, their different nature and function. It is not an external feature that Goethe's Mephistopheles should belong entirely to the objective world, while here (as already in Dostoyevsky) he is only a projection of the hero's mind. This follows from the situation we have already described where the new Faust enacts his tragedy in the study. The former Faust forsakes his study in order to conquer the whole of reality, the 'small world' as well as the 'great'. His story thus becomes the story of humanity and the world. The powers with whom he wrestles and who struggle for his soul are objective powers of an objective reality—human society. So, too, therefore, Mephistopheles. His black magic, his sorcery, as I showed in my *Faust* essays, are only formally phantastic. In content they are just as real and effective a force in social reality as Faust himself, as his deeds and the people whom these affect, and of which both they and he are the victims.

It is a different matter when these deeds are confined within the walls of the study. This is already the case with Ivan Karamazov. The parricide in Dostoyevsky is essentially a psychological and moral reality, more an experiment with oneself, an inner school of self-examination and self-knowledge than a brute fact of the outside world. (This is already so with Raskolnikov's real murder, as is abundantly clear if one compares his psychology, ethics and behaviour with the related model of Balzac's Rastignac.) Mann's study-type of Faustus thus inevitably and organically entails a certain likeness in treatment which extends in places to the physical appearance of the devil.

Intellectually and artistically, however, this likeness is purely external, unfundamental. It would be wrong to speak of 'influence'. The convergence is dictated by kindred tendencies of the period. But once more the differences are more important than the occasional simillarities. Dostoyevsky posed the problem in psychological and ethical terms. Hence the relationship between Ivan Karamazov and his devil—despite the complicated see-sawing between reality and vision—is extremely simple. Ivan says all there is to say to his tormentor and tempter: 'You are the embodiment of myself, though you only stand for one side of me ... of my thoughts and feelings—the most disgusting, the stupidest side ...' The above and the down-under, Heaven and Hell, are quite separate from one another in the world which Dostoyevsky wishes to present. True, the actual structure of his world is dialectically complex and goes far beyond this relatively simple moral and metaphysical dualism. Nevertheless it is this dualism which dominates Karamazov's relationship with his devil: the devil embodies his psychological and moral under-world.

The same goes for Adrian Leverkühn's devil—how else would he be a devil, his devil? However, the underworld in Thomas Mann's imperialist Faustian world is quite different from, more complicated than, the world of the Karamazov tragedy. In the first place, to start with perhaps the most important factor, this devil is but a principle of release; he sets free existing mental energies: 'Where nothing is there, the devil too has lost his right.... We make naught new—that is other people's matter. We only release, only set free. We let the lameness and self-consciousness, the chaste scruples and doubts go to the Devil. We physic away fatigue merely by a little charm—hyperaemia, the great and the small, of the person and of the time.' This is why the devil of this Faust world is 'the true lord of inspiration' —a morbid, inhuman, anti-human inspiration.

Mann's devil knows quite well that he is talking of historical matter, of the cultural situation of the present. He describes the human condition of the artist in a way which frequently echoes Tonio Kröger's confessions: 'The artist is the brother of the criminal and the madman . . . morbid and healthy! Without the morbid would life all its whole life never have survived.' And in the same sense he says to Adrian: 'A general chilling of your life and your relations to men lies in the nature of things— rather it lies already in your nature. . . .' But here again, of course, it is the differences which are important. Tonio Kröger and Gustav Aschenbach see something universal, supra-historical in their own personal fate. The devil of the new Faustus knows better: he mocks Adrian by referring to Goethe: 'That is it, you do not think of the passage of time, you do not think historic-ally, when you complain that such and such a one could have it "wholly", joys and pains endlessly, without the hour-glass being set for him, the reckoning finally made. What he in his classical decades could have without us, certainly, that nowadays we alone have to offer.' His mockery goes further still, empha-sizing not only Goethe's lack of diabolism but pointing out what is specifically modern in that which he offers: 'And we offer better, we offer only the right and true—that is no longer the classical, my friend, what we give to experience, it is the archaic, the primeval, that which long since has not been tried. Who knows today, who even knew in classical times, what in-spiration is, what genuine, old, primeval enthusiasm, insicklied by critique, unparalysed by thought or by the mortal domina-tion of reason—who knows the divine raptus?' He rejects contemptuously the idea of the devil as the guardian of criti-cism; on the contrary, he is the patron of uninhibited irrationalist intuition.

To complete the comparison, Tonio Kröger and Aschenbach longed to achieve self-contained works—and did so. They suf-fered for them, sacrificed their personal well-being. But no matter how problematic their lives they never doubted the work of art itself. But for Leverkühn the situation is a different one— and so it is for his historically-minded devil who can put his finger on what is specifically contemporary in the contemporary situation. He says of modern art: 'Does not production threaten to come to an end? And whatever of serious stuff gets on to paper betrays effort and distaste.' The devil dismisses the external 'social grounds' of this situation as superficial. The real causes, he says, lie deeper: 'Composing itself has got too hard, devilishly hard. Where work does not go any longer with sincerity how is one to work?' He expands this idea: 'What I do not deny is a certain general satisfaction which the state of the "work" generally vouchsafes me. I am against works, by and large. Why should I not find some pleasure in the sickness which has attacked the idea of the musical work! ... The historical movement of the musical material has turned against the self-contained work.... The subsumption of expression under a reconciling universal is the innermost principle of the musical illusion. It is all up with it. The claim to consider the general harmonically contained in the particular contradicts itself. It is all up with the once bindingly valid conventions, which guaranteed the freedom of play.' And in the same connection he calls Adrian's parodistic tendencies a melancholy 'aristocratic nihilism'. Thus what for Tonio Kröger and Aschenbach was the only fixed point is itself held up for question here.

The devil then manifests the whole inner being of Adrian Leverkühn, not merely his bad qualities, as in the case of Ivan Karamazov. The underworld of the mature imperialist age embraces the sum of the modern artist's inner life. True, Leverkühn like Ivan Karamazov recoils before the horrid shape in which the devil appears. But there is a difference. This devil here is the caricature concentration of imperialist self-destruction, of the disintegration of man and work, of the artist's self-annihilation. Yet he materializes in a life which is devoted to nothing but art, a life which strangles its own humanity for the sake of art. But the art is made perfect only to destroy itself, to kill art as such and the work of art.

Hence the devil is right to say of hell: 'It is at bottom only a continuation of the extravagant existence.' And he also knows: 'It is that extravagant living, the only one that suffices a proud

75

soul. Your arrogance will probably never want to exchange with a lukewarm one.' The hell of this Faustus is no more supernatural, no less the world of modern (bourgeois) man than for earlier writers, such as Dostoyevsky, Strindberg or Shaw, who criticized the self-destructive nature of the bourgeoisie of our day. But this hell is more exclusive. It concentrates on what is noblest and best, on what seems to be the most timeless, the most violently anti-contemporary, anti-bourgeois.

It would be idle to seek a real-life model for Mann's Faustus. If anyone, he distantly resembles the ascetic figure of Nietzsche, withdrawn yet craving life, shy of the world yet dictatorially unbending. (There are echoes in the story itself which cannot be accidental.) More important, however, is the fact that in outlook there is much of the decadent, pre-fascist essence of Nietzscheanism in him. Many decades ago Stefan George wrote a poem on Nietzsche's tragedy, as he understood it. George posed a solution: 'It should have sung, this new soul . . .' But this avoids understanding what Nietzsche's tragedy really was. Yet inadvertently it provides some kind of motto to this novel. For Thomas Mann shows what kind of a song Nietzsche might have sung had he lived in the contemporary world—the theme, the form, the pathos and the parody. Mann, more critical than George because he is a humanist, fulfils the song and demonstrates the tragedy.

Mann's devil is thus a historical critic of the entire bourgeois culture of imperialism. Here again Leverkühn is closely related to his familiar spirit. He, too, in his thought and work, is a historical critic of his age. When his purest and most timid attempt to get a little closer to life breaks down with the terrible death of his young nephew, Leverkühn has the following exchange with his friend: ' "I find," he said, "that it is not to be." "What, Adrian, is not to be?" "The good and the noble," he answered me; "what we call the human, although it is good, and noble. What human beings have fought for and stormed citadels, what the ecstatics exultantly announced—that is not to be. It will be taken back.

I will take it back." "I don't quite understand, dear man. What will you take back?" "The Ninth Symphony," he replied.'

This throws into relief the decisive issue. According to Adrian, as he has explained much earlier, it is here that the new music achieves its intellectual and cultural victory. 'It has emancipated her from the sphere of a small-town specialism and piping and brought her into contact with the great world of the mind, the general artistic and intellectual movement of the time.... All that proceeds from the Beethoven of the last period and his polyphony....' This is why it is so important that Leverkühn's friend and biographer writes of Adrian's last work, a Faust symphony: 'He wrote it, no doubt, with an eye on Beethoven's Ninth, as its counterpart in a most melancholy sense of the word.' And since this forms the intellectual and creative climax to Leverkühn's work he must make sure that his retraction of all the good and noble in man's development is done with a clear consciousness and at a high artistic level. This work is thus a triumph for the devil.

But that is not the last word, either of the novel or of Leverkühn. In his last, late, tragic moment of insight and self-criticism which occurs just before his mental eclipse, he holds judgment upon the devil, upon his self-destruction at the hands of a devilish productivity, upon his aristocratic nihilism: ' "Yes verily, dear mates, that art is stuck and grown too heavy and scorneth itselfe and God's poor man knoweth no longer where to turn in his sore plight, that is belike the fault in the times. But if one invite the devil as guest, to pass beyond all this and get to the breakthrough, he chargeth his soul and taketh the guilt of the time upon his own shoulders, so that he is damned. For it hath been said "Be sober, and watch!" But that is not the affair of some; rather, instead of shrewdly concerning themselves with what is needful upon earth that it may be better there, and discreetly doing it, that among men such order shall be stablished that again for the beautiful work living soil and true harmony be prepared, man playeth the truant and breaketh out in hellish drunkenness; so giveth he his soul thereto and cometh among the carrion." '

III

With Adrian Leverkühn's last words the tragedy of a musician turns not simply into the tragedy of music, art, culture in the age of imperialism (this relationship existed, as I showed, from the outset.) It becomes simultaneously the tragedy of Germany, indeed the whole of bourgeois humanity today.

But this connection, too, is only the culmination of a maturing consciousness and self-consciousness. Implicitly, it is there from the start. Moreover, it determines the whole epic form of the work. At the end what existed only in-itself exists for-itself. This climax of consciousness is simultaneously the intellectual and artistic justification of the structure and the principles of composition.

The form which this connection takes is very individual, and we must examine it a little further because of its apparent resemblance to modern stylistic developments in the novel. Mann's essential difference and distance from them comes out quite clearly. The real question is the treatment of time, for here the modernists have indulged in the wildest orgies. However, their experiments, which one may condemn as empty, artificial, hothouse, do reflect something of the relationship of the individual and his personal life to the social framework or, more precisely, historical time of which this particular life is a moment. The reflection may be distorted, mannered, playful indeed, but reflection it is.

Obviously, this problem could only be raised after literature had become consciously historical, that is, after the revolutionary innovations of Scott (for this turning-point see my *Historical Novel*[1]). But though deeply modified the novel kept its traditional

[1] Merlin Press, 1962.

narrative manner for quite some time. For it is only historicity, that is historical time which Scott made artistically conscious. And yet individual life was here at its most truthful and concrete. Seen as a moment in history, it did not as yet become problematic. The novelist could experience and represent individual and historical time as an inseparable unity. An individual's rise and decline was an organic part of social and historical rise and decline; it corresponded to objective reality. Whatever the stylistic differences and whatever their historical and particular causes, it is this way of looking at things which prevails in *War and Peace* and even *Buddenbrooks*.

The difficulty occurs when novelists come to concentrate on the meaninglessness of individual life, say from *L'Education Sentimentale* onwards. Obviously if one looks on both social and personal life as pointless and sees reality revealed in the inevitable and wretched failure of the best human aspirations, then time, too, and its presentation must assume a new function. Time appears as no longer the natural, objective and historical medium in which men move and develop. It is distorted into a dead and deadening outward power. The passage of time is the frame within which a person suffers degradation. It turns into an independent and remorseless machine which flattens, levels and destroys all personal plans and wishes, all singularity, personality itself. And if in some of the most modern writers we find a kindlier attitude to time, within a similar general outlook, this is but a sign that their despair, pessimism and irrationalism have taken on a playful and frivolous character.

This distortion of experience occurs in late capitalism; it is especially a product of the social reality of imperialism. Not before then can the rupture between individual (experienced) and objective (physical and historical) time take place and be made conscious. The concepts of this break have been worked out in modern philosophy from Bergson and Dilthey to Heidegger and Sartre. But individual differences of attitude have no interest for us, since they are all confined within the general opposition of objective and subjective time. In literature all the formal innovations in the novel of the imperialist period, particularly since the First World War, have been dominated by this view of time.

We cannot possibly enumerate, analyse or evaluate here the variants of this new attitude. The main thing is what they have in common. And the most important factor here is the destruction of the unity and process of epic totality. If the opposition between experienced and real time is stressed, if the differences in tempo between them (where experience turns minutes into eternities and years into brief moments) are made into principles of composition to 'prove' the deadness, inferiority or unreality of objective time, then the whole crumbles under the excessive weight of the moments. This game with fragments of experience in subjective time (considered as the only real time) sometimes goes so far that the only thread on which a writer can assemble his heterogeneous bits is their subjective duration. Any gradation of importance in objective reality is simply dismissed. In Flaubert subjective experience was still the victim of a hard reality. Here it hypertrophies; from its 'own', 'sovereign' resources it creates a more suitable 'universe'. But this triumph of subjectivity is only the measure of its real impotence and insignificance. The more or less genuine writers of our day are to some extent aware of this situation. But they, too, are ruled by the sentiments and attitudes (and hence ideologies) endemic to imperialism. Hence they look upon this impotence and insignificance of an apparently sovereign subjective world and an apparently 'real' time as the only positive thing possible, as the only way of being entirely true to life, as the only real substance and content of the world. This, they would say, is our 'cosmic' condition. Thereby, they canonize this extreme subjective distortion of reality. In it they find a fitting expression of a distorted world which in their eyes forms the foundation of all reality.

It is difficult indeed for a modern writer to escape such influences, even when he has a relatively clear and sober view of their destructive effect on literary form. We are not thinking here of any so-called irresistible techniques or literary fashions. A true writer can resist these easily enough. The tendencies we are describing come from life itself, from the writer's own life. A writer who really wishes to catch the historical peculiarity of our day cannot pass them by with impunity. Of course, the peculiarity we are dealing with is not objective. It is not the real stamp of our epoch, but a distorted reflection inevitably produced by certain social and historical circumstances. What is at issue here is not the objective, social reality of our time (or for that matter the life of mankind as such, all 'cosmic' being). This is no inextricable chaos, no hopeless labyrinth of distortion. The point is that this reality inevitably appears thus to many people, in particular to the artistically and philosophically minded, in general to an intelligentsia estranged from the objective driving forces of society.

The imperialist age as such is the epoch of world wars and world revolutions. The tendencies which prepare the wars are objective; they operate in the economic and cultural spheres, in internal and foreign politics. They end in chaos and blood, warping all that is human in individuals, classes and nations. Their power is considerable, as has been proved by two world wars, twelve years of National Socialism in Germany, etc.

Yet whatever this power (which today is once more on the march, gathering strength, recruiting, spreading and concentrating), it is not fatally irresistible. Proof of this is the existence for more than thirty years of the Soviet Union, the struggle of the Popular Front against Fascism, the victory over Hitler Germany in the Second World War, the rise of the Peoples' Democracies, the growing resistance to imperialism in both the 'metropolitan' countries and the colonies. Thus whatever its immediate features of chaos and distortion, the essential trend of our epoch is towards a meaningful future, an ordered and cultured world fit for individuals and nations.

But this is not so easy to recognize. For those still trapped in the insoluble contradictions of a nineteenth century

Weltanschauung; for those who yield or subscribe to the reactionary pseudo-solutions ceaselessly produced by the arbitrary bourgeois thought of the imperialist period; for all such the world
will remain an inhuman chaos, distorted and distorting. And this
indeed is how the world is viewed by the so-called *avant-garde*
of the bourgeois intelligentsia. One is faced with a curious
phenomenon. Under Hitler the official ideology of reaction declared demagogic war upon an alleged threat of barbarism. Today
it does so again with a crusading cry. But the 'order' which is
hereby proclaimed only appears orderly and harmonious in the
worst, mass-produced literary and philosophic best-sellers. Should
a genuine, sincere artist start from the same or related premises—
or simply be influenced by them—he will create a picture of
chaos, a world with a dual conception of time: objective and
dead on the one hand, subjective, living and uniquely true on
the other.

This, then, is an indispensable note in any composition which
takes its theme from the bourgeois world in the imperialist age
and seeks to be truthful and comprehensive. But one can distinguish here between the really great writer and the merely
talented, whatever his gifts. The great writer has his heart in the
right place; he is sensitive to new impressions, but can always
tell the difference between reality and appearance, between the
objective character of the world and its (however inevitably) distorted reflection.

So Thomas Mann. He distinguishes himself sharply from his
contemporaries in his treatment of the problem of time. For
instance, *The Magic Mountain*: the experience and measurement
of time differ considerably for the world above (the sanatorium)
and the world below (everyday bourgeois reality). Both the
characters and Mann himself spend much time analysing time.
But Mann is quite conscious—and so, therefore, is the reader at
every step of the leisurely narrative—that the magic mountain
belongs in real time, that only its inhabitants (and then only in
their imagination) regard it as a reality-in-itself, as an isolated,

self-subsisting world with a time-scheme of its own. The magic mountain is isolated for objective, medical reasons. As Mann shows, all the social influences of the people, all that has conditioned their lives 'below' persists unchanged here. If there has been any modification, then indeed it is simply that the social behaviour which the people have brought with them has been allowed to develop in pure conditions. People have quite literally more time up here. For this reason problems which otherwise would have remained unconscious can here become conscious (Castorp-Settembrini-Naphta). And for the same reason the stupidity and philistinism of people can sink lower than 'down below' (e.g. the quagmire atmosphere of the second half). The curious problem of time, therefore, is just as objective here as it is 'below', and as it would be in any 'normal' novel. Thomas Mann uses a modern technique as *one* means of characterization. He treats what is subjective as subjective and can thereby let it take its place in an objective narrative world.

This comes out even more clearly in *Dr. Faustus*. Thomas Mann employs a double time-sequence with extraordinary subtlety. On the one hand we have Adrian Leverkühn's career, starting with his youth before the First World War and ending with his insanity and death in 1940. On the other we are constantly made aware, by Leverkühn's friend and biographer, the schoolmaster Serenus Zeitblom, of the times in which the life of his immortal comrade and master are set down, and of which we become more aware as the novel proceeds. Thus the period of fascism which Leverkühn could not consciously experience, the second imperialist world war with its quick initial victories and terrible defeats—these surround the tragedy of the protagonist like a chorus. The two time-scales, the two separate periods of time continually intertwine and shed light on one another.

This last observation shows where Thomas Mann differs from his *avant-garde* contemporaries. For if these two periods of time —that of the biography and that of the biographer—can throw light on one another, it is because they are objective. Both in reality and in the novel they form one unified time sequence. If they are separated, it is only to bring out certain factors which connect them objectively and which could not be highlighted in a simple biography, at least not artistically. Thus Thomas Mann's apparent use of a modern 'multiple time' only reinforces (though in a complicated, roundabout way) the 'traditional' realist treatment of time as a social and historical unity.

IV

What is the intellectual and artistic content of this unity? Clearly the relationship between Adrian Leverkühn's work and the tragedy of the German people in the imperialist age.

The relationship is conveyed artistically through the figure of the biographer, Serenus Zeitblom. The hero himself, Adrian Leverkühn, is too shut-off, too shut-up within himself to be the focus of such connections. On its own his biography would be incomplete; it would bear no relationship to the world. Indeed, the more complete one tried to make it, the less it would have to do with the world; the more, indeed, it would fail as biography. All we should have was Adrian and his exclusive concern with his art. Yet Adrian's art is instinct with the problems of his time, shaped and determined by them. What Thomas Mann does, therefore, is to bring in the biographer, put him and his personality in the foreground and let him point out the connections, which thereby are enabled to play an essential part in the work.

The two time-sequences show how often Adrian is the unconscious accomplice of his age even when he most arrogantly supposes he had nothing to do with it. But it is not so much Zeitblom's analysis and narration which bring this out as Zeitblom's actual life.

Serenus, much more than his friend (the new Faustus banished to the 'small world' of the study), is a Raabe figure. Even his

name has a Raabe-like ring. His classical education, wide knowledge, old-fashioned humanism; his timidity combined with
shrewdness; his devotion to his seven-stringed viola-d'amore
which he plays with modest virtuosity in his leisure hours—all
this brings him closer to the Raabe world and atmosphere than
any previous character in Mann. And then his attitude to the
times, which we shall deal with more closely in a moment. Here
all we wish to point out is the critical sense which lurks behind
the outer lack of worldliness and which is yet powerless to resist
(even inwardly) the tendencies to fascism. How similar to the
actual Raabe characters who criticized yet could not resist Bismarck, both before and after he had established himself! It is
Zeitblom then who gives this modern and universal tragedy a
provincial, old-fashioned, typically German stamp. Fascism, of
course, in its modern German, imperialist form, plays an important part in the novel, indeed determines its intellectual and moral
content. But the immediate surface of life is the old Germany
which either accommodates itself to the new reaction or proves
unable to withstand its assault. The highest intellectual achievements of imperialist Germany find their natural habitat in this
atmosphere. We can study them closely and watch their oscilla-
tion between accommodation and impotence.

Serenus Zeitblom is an 'intermediary figure'. His function is
to lay bare the moral background of this impotence in the best
German middle class intellectuals—best, that is, in the sense of
culture and interests. Zeitblom is a humanist of the old school.
He is repelled by any appeal to the 'underworld'. Hence his attitude to his friend's music is a mixture of excitement, enthusiasm,
admiration and deepest distrust. This feeling never leaves him.
It is with him as he listens to all those fascinating discussions
of the inter-war years which, in their irresponsible, frivolous
manner, prepared the ideology of fascism on 'a high intellectual
level'. The same feeling determines his attitude to the Hitler
regime, too.

Thomas Mann chooses an 'intermediary figure', a type of the

old Germany. Yet he is by no means a run-of-the-mill intellectual philistine. In his quaint *a' la Raabe* manner he combines a gullible acceptance of every official proclamation, an ability to adapt his language and thought to each and every government requirement with considerable insight into the contradictions which have ruled German society and thought over these decades. This, for instance, is how he records a new and apparently successful development in Hitler's submarine warfare: 'We owe this success to a new torpedo of fabulous properties which German technicians have succeeded in constructing, and I cannot repress a certain satisfaction over our ever alert spirit of invention, our national gift of not being swerved aside by however many setbacks. It stands wholly at the service of the regime which brought us into this war, laid the Continent literally at our feet and replaced the intellectual's dream of a European Germany with the upsetting, rather brittle reality, intolerable, so it seems to the rest of the world, of a German Europe.' One can find many similar comments.

At times, however, Zeitblom is able to glimpse the general laws of social development in a way quite beyond the best average German intellectual. For example, his judgment of the situation of Germany in the First World War. Emotionally, he shares all the illusions of August 1914, the longing for a breakthrough 'to a higher form of communal life'. Yet he adds: 'Ethically speaking, the only way a people can achieve a higher form of communal life is not by a foreign war, but by a civil one—even with bloodshed.'

This sentiment is more forcefully expressed in his fury over the meeting of Hitler and Mussolini in Florence where they pose as defenders of culture against the Bolshevik menace. He has indeed 'a natural horror of radical revolution and the dictatorship of the lower classes', but he adds: 'Bolshevism to my knowledge has never destroyed any works of art. That was far more within the sphere of activity of those who assert that they are protecting us from it.' And between these remarks there is a very interesting confession, certainly quite uncommon for the Germany of the time: 'my notions about mob rule take on another colour, and the dictatorship of the proletariat begins to seem to me, a German burgher, an ideal situation compared with the now possible one of the dictatorship of the scum of the earth.'

These contradictions throw a deep light into the mental chaos which ferments beneath the cultivated humanism and carefully chosen words. In 1918 he recognizes that the epoch of bourgeois humanism has come to an end. He sees the connection between this crisis and fascism. 'It is true that certain strata of bourgeois democracy seemed and seem today ripe for what I termed the dictatorship of the scum: willing to make common cause with it to linger out their privileges.' But these insights have no consequence, not even for his own intellectual outlook.

His recluse friend Adrian has fewer illusions in these matters. In 1914 he is cool towards the 'breakthrough' fever: 'It would not help much if I did understand, for at present, anyhow, the crude event will just make our shut-inness and shut-offness more complete, however far your military swarm into Europe.' Or again, in a short, but extremely interesting conversation with his friend on freedom. Adrian, following his general artistic beliefs, speaks of the sterility which freedom (the 'destroyed conventions') inevitably entails. (We quoted some of these remarks earlier with reference to art.) He replies to Serenus's objections by exploring the inner dialectic of freedom, as he understands it: 'But freedom is, of course, another word for subjectivity, and some fine day she does not hold out any longer, some time or other she despairs of the possibility of being creative out of herself and seeks shelter and security in the objective. Freedom always inclines to dialectic reversals. She realizes herself very soon in constraint, fulfils herself in the subordination to law, rule, coercion, system—but to fulfil herself therein does not mean, therefore, she ceases to be freedom.' Serenus rejects this dialectical reversal: 'But actually she is no longer freedom, as little as dictatorship born out of revolution is still freedom.' 'Are you sure of it?' retorts Adrian briefly, and for the rest of the conversation turns from politics to purely musical problems.

What we learn of Adrian's attitude to his time is very sparse. Still less do we see how deeply such flashes of insight affect his whole conduct. His actual compositions reveal very little. Adrian's self-absorption and hostility towards social problems, his deliberate blindness to the surrounding world form one of his most important traits of character. It is all the more significant then that Mann should very skilfully lift the curtain here and there. For, as we have shown and will show further, Leverkühn's attitude to the social and historical reality of his time does, in fact, play the decisive part in his tragic fall.

To approach this in the right way let us go back to Serenus. We said that the dominant feature of his attitude to the world was his defencelessness before the assault of reactionary ideology, mounted before 1914, intellectually fortified between 1918 and 1933 and finally let loose in the rabble-rousing horrors of national socialism. The defencelessness of the schoolmaster Zeitblom is typical precisely because he is not an average figure. We have touched upon the above-average character of his views. He proves his above-average moral character by retiring when Hitler comes to power. He refuses to be involved in the 'educational' branch of Goebbels's propaganda. His complete estrangement from his two Nazi sons demonstrates his intransigence towards Hitler's regime.

Where then is his defencelessness? Precisely here.

Thomas Mann frequently introduces his lonely Adrian into intellectual company, starting with the theology students of Halle and culminating in the various *avant-garde* circles of his Munich period. What do we see here? In every case the mental and emotional reflexes of a crisis in which bourgeois democracy, born of the revolutions of the seventeenth and eighteenth centuries, now finds itself; a crisis which Serenus described as the end of bourgeois humanism.

We cannot go into all these attitudes here. It is enough to say that Mann allows us to glimpse, in these conversations, the most important trends in German pre-fascist thinking and in the ideology which prepared fascism itself; just as, with the same skill he is able to bring to life for us all the essential tendencies in modern music. The moral atmosphere of these discussions is particularly significant. The student symposium is still redolent of idealistic conviction which, however confused, is sincere. Nevertheless, all the themes of later reaction are sounded here: the arrogant rejection of economic solutions to social problems as 'shallow', touching only the surface of human existence; the equally arrogant repudiation of all questions and answers based on reason and the understanding; the *a priori* acceptance of the 'irrational' as something higher, more fundamental, beyond reason and understanding; above all, the fetish of the *Volk* with all its (then still unconscious) aggressively chauvinistic implications, which still took the 'purely intellectual' form of the natural superiority of the Germanic to both East and West, the 'purely intellectual' belief in Germany's mission as world saviour.

Adrian Leverkühn has a few minor skirmishes with this ideology. But Serenus Zeitblom, for whom it is thoroughly alien, who indeed as a still unshaken humanist should quite oppose it, remains an interested listener. And this happens again in the *avant-garde* circles which gather after the first defeat of imperialist Germany. The reactionary tendencies are more conscious now. Indeed the whole atmosphere has changed. An aesthetic and moral snobbery now holds sway, frivolous and irresponsible, sympathizing with every reactionary and pseudo-modernist trend. Zeitblom is deeply distrustful of this milieu and its intellectual attitudes. Inwardly, he is well aware of the reason for his distrust. He describes his feelings as he hears democracy, reason, the heritage of the nineteenth century besmirched and violence, dictatorship extolled to universal acclamation: 'Of course one may say so; only one might, for my taste, dealing with this description of a mounting barbarism, have said so with rather more fear and trembling and rather less blithe satisfaction.'

He correctly sums up the essential tendency of the milieu as 'deliberate rebarbarization'. In a letter from Adrian of this period he senses—and this is very important—'how near aestheticism and barbarism are to each other, aestheticism as the herald of barbarism'; it is something which he has 'experienced in his very soul'. Nevertheless, even in these discussions Serenus remains an interested but largely silent listener; only when it comes to music does he every now and then entertain the company with his performance of forgotten old composers on his viola-d'amore. He remarks of Breisacher, an *avant-garde* philosopher whom he finds particularly repulsive, that one could dispute his facts and question his mixing of the *avant-garde* with the reactionary. 'But a sensitive man does not like to disturb another; it is unpleasant to break in on a train of thought with logical or historical objections; even in the anti-intellectual such a man respects and spares the intellectual.' Only once does he attempt to stand up in defence of investigation and truth, but his remarks fall flat. And Serenus adds self-critically that they were permeated with 'an idealism ... well known to the point of being bad taste and merely embarrassing to the new ideas.' Later indeed he realizes the error that lies hidden here: 'that it was the mistake of our civilization to have practised all too magnanimously this respect and forbearance. For we found after all that the opposite side met us with sheer impudence and the most determined intolerance.'

So we find in Serenus that intellectual and moral division which is most obvious in his attitude to Hitlerism. He expresses this inner conflict quite openly when he speaks of Germany's defeat: 'No, surely I did not want it, and yet—I have been driven to want it, I wish for it today and will welcome it. ... For liars and lickspittles mixed us a poison draught and took away our senses. We drank—for we Germans perennially yearn for intoxication—and under its spell, through years of deluded highliving, we committed a superfluity of shameful deeds, which must now be paid for.'

But this division is more than a mental conflict. It means that Zeitblom is inwardly tied to that 'national community' whose basic direction he must hate and despise; that he is spiritually bound to the ideological tendencies of which we have just heard him speak. Whatever his criticism, insights, reservations this bond is the human and moral foundation of the defencelessness of the best German intellectuals in face of the fascist domination of their thoughts and feelings.

Why this defencelessness? Whence this impotence of insight, conviction and sentiment? To resist, two closely connected factors are needed. First, an Archimedean point from which one can view the fascist trend *from outside*; an Archimedean point from which, whenever necessary, one can *act* against it. This objective possibility of action will then turn words and thoughts of resistance into deeds. Serenus cannot find this point. Settembrini in *The Magic Mountain* was still proof against Naphta's ideology even if he was powerless against his sophistry. But then Settembrini was not a German. Nor was he in any doubt about the bourgeois humanism on which he based his support for capitalism. Hence his vigour and ineffectualness. The German Zeitblom is free of the Italian's illusions. Intellectually, this may seem a step forward, but in practice, in the actual clash of ideas, it constitutes a graver weakness.

The first phase of impotence here passes into the second. Serenus can find nothing positive to pit against the new intellectual world in which he clearly recognizes reaction and barbarism. In objecting he feels that he intrudes, that it behoves him better to keep quiet—which he does. Thomas Mann has described this reaction before. It is the stance of the 'gentleman from Rome' who resists Cipolla's mass hypnosis by honourably doing nothing. He is powerless because, as the author of *Mario and the Magician* remarks, he acts from pure negativity; he simply does not want to submit to the hypnosis. But mere not wanting is too flimsy; it turns unnoticeably into acceptance and then surrender. All Serenus Zeitblom's complicated thoughts, moral reservations, aesthetic analyses, etc., only make explicit (speaking generally) what is implicit in the dumb refusal of the 'gentleman from Rome'. Serenus has no Archimedean point outside the intellectual life of Germany which is headed irresistibly towards barbarism. He has no positive ideal which he might hold up to the uncertain longing, the intellectual clowning or the plain Hitlerite devilry of reaction.

But this is simply to describe the impotence. What are its origins? Here the problem of the 'small world' comes up again, this time on its social side. But it takes us back to Leverkühn's artistic development, his devil's pact, his servitude to the devil in his work. Enough has been said to see that behind Leverkühn's creative problems stands the question of freedom and belonging, subjectivity and order. Like Serenus, Adrian realizes that subjectivity and freedom have reached a crisis. We have already studied his views on this matter. From earliest youth he believes that 'a silly order is better than no order at all'.

Hence he has always striven to conquer freedom and subjectivity. Yet he has always been thrown back again on himself as much as the most consciously and deliberately subjective artist. His conquest of the capricious is purely formal; his 'order' and 'reason' are cold, fabricated. He despises the emotions, the 'cow warmth' of music. His art is bitter and parodistic. His cult of reason and order turns into a glittering obscurantism. Serenus criticizes this tendency rightly: 'The rationalism you call for has a good deal of superstition about it—of belief in the incomprehensibly and vaguely daemonic, the kind of thing we have in games of chance, fortune-telling with cards, and shaking dice. Contrary to what you say, your system seems to me more calculated to dissolve human reason in magic.' (Hence his pact with the devil and the devilish in his art; it is a forced solution.) How does this complex problem connect with the 'small world'? Adrian is much clearer about this than his critical, humanist friend. He says in a conversation: 'Isn't it amusing that music for a long time considered herself a means of release, whereas she herself, like all the arts, needed to be redeemed from a pompous isolation, which was the fruit of the culture-emancipation, the elevation of culture, as a substitute for religion—from being alone with an élite of culture, called the 'public', which will soon no longer be, which even now no longer is, so that soon art will be entirely alone, alone to die, unless she were to find her way to the 'people', that is, to say it unromantically, to human beings?' One notices that the word 'people' is put in quotation marks. Adrian is quite consistent. He has talked about 'order' in just the same way (even a silly order, he says, even a criminal and reactionary order, German history would add), preferring it to freedom and subjectivity.

The real people, their real life, their real wishes are ignored. Hence the problem posed by the crisis of bourgeois democracy and its ideological reflection, bourgeois humanism; the question put by life, the social life of Germany, to mankind is distorted. The only answer which is sought and found is a purely ideological or artistic one. This distortion, this reduction to the purely formal and abstract is the main intellectual and moral component of the impotence of which we have been speaking. The actual 'order' which National Socialism brings about is, of course, no abstraction, but corresponds very precisely and specifically to the needs of the most reactionary brand of monopoly capitalism, satisfying these in every respect, not least by its conquest of freedom and subjectivity. Yet there is another kind of order in society which opposes this, another way of conquering outworn freedoms, subjectivity and caprice (i.e., the anarchy, free competition, exploitation, etc., of capitalism), in a word the working-class and its revolution, however little striking power it may have at a given moment, however confused many workers may be.

These are the battlefields of our time. It is on these that bourgeois humanism must be overcome and a new humanism arise. It is not our task here to show why between 1914 and 1945 popular opposition to reaction in Germany suffered so many

93

defeats. The important thing here to notice is that this whole struggle simply did not exist for the intellectual type Adrian-Serenus. In their thought and work they remained lifelong prisoners of the 'small world' of the study. They saw the people only as the object of various demagogies, only in quotation marks. The antithesis between freedom and order, however deeply, however artistically they may have experienced it, remained for them an abstract, ideological-cum-aesthetic opposition. For this reason their purely intellectual, purely artistic, purely formal search for 'order in general' very naturally and inevitably acquires as its content the *results* of those great social struggles, that reality, that real antagonism to which they paid no attenion. Their insights are right but abstract; they are measured on a 'world-historical scale'. Hence neither Serenus nor Adrian can find an Archimedean point from which to withstand the tide of reaction. They have no positive ideal to set against a reactionary ideology. Serenus becomes a passively hostile observer of barbarism. Adrian Leverkühn, the honest ascetic, absorbs into his work all the dehumanizing *motifs* of the age preceding and culminating in fascism; these, indeed, come to form his essential artistic foundation.

The tragedy of the 'small world', its art and culture here reaches a climax. The retreat into the study had been forced on the best intellectuals. Bourgeois humanism foundered because those democratic ideals which from Rabelais to Robespierre had been the public concern of all progressive men in every field—political, social, cultural, artistic—no longer played their vanguard rôle, but had been pressed into the service of conservatism and hypocrisy. The cultural intelligentsia fled from this situation into the 'small world' of the study. Originally, the aim was to save their ideals from pollution in the unaccustomed struggles of the modern world; in intention therefore an act of opposition. However, the more the 'small world' closed in upon them, the more this hermetic seclusion became their sole reality, all the more powerfully did the reactionary tendencies of the capitalist world exert a subterranean pressure upon their problems and solutions, upon what seemed to them a purely inward activity. They were not altogether unaware of this subterranean influence. But from their seclusion they inevitably distorted its real nature. It became the cult of the unconscious, depth psychology, myth-making of the inner life, etc. In all these forms, in all their philosophical and artistic variants, the intelligentsia crippled its spiritual existence.

Speaking generally, this development is an international one. But Germany plays a special, tragi-grotesque, preferential role. Germany's humanism from the sixteenth to eighteenth centuries had never been anything more than an ideology in a backward country. At most it was a purely intellectual preparation for a democratic revolution which never materialized, which never transformed the social structure as in France and England. Thus Germany accommodated itself to imperialism and the German intelligentsia found itself pushed into the 'small world' of pure inwardness, never having experienced bourgeois humanism as the culture of a whole social life. As Marx wrote prophetically more than a hundred years ago: 'Germany will therefore one day find itself on the level of European decay without ever having stood on the level of European emancipation.'

For this reason both the ideological disintegration of bourgeois humanism as well as the, at first, subterranean, then rapid and conscious drive to decadence and reaction occurs in a purer and more complete form in Germany than in any other country. It is no accident that the leaders of the muses of modern reaction, Schopenhauer and Wagner, Nietzsche and Freud, Heidegger and Klages are without exception Germans, international leaders in a much larger sense than the reactionary ideologists of other nations. The political and social reaction of the world acquires its highest (so far), its 'classical' form in Hitler's Germany. In this way the so typically German, the Raabe-cum-Kaiseraschern tragedy of Adrian Leverkühn is the typical tragedy of modern bourgeois art and intellect.

It is again no accident that this tragedy was written by a German, Thomas Mann. No other writer has suffered so much from either the Germanic or the bourgeois. No-one has wrestled so unremittingly with the problems that have sprung from these closely-connected spheres. True, he is hardly more able than his own characters to paint a picture of the real forces which oppose the devilish in the life and culture of the people, both liberated and still struggling for liberation. The intellectual *dramatis personae* of his writing are the disintegrating bourgeois humanism and the reactionary, mystifying, demagogic powers which utilize this disintegration on behalf of monopoly capitalism. But since he has thought through this tragedy more deeply and experienced it more painfully than any of his bourgeois contemporaries, what he sees on the horizon is enough artistically to give his conflict a conclusive and comprehensive *finale*.

Many years ago Thomas Mann wrote: 'It would be well with Germany, I repeat, she would have found herself, as soon as Karl Marx shall have read Friedrich Hölderlin. Such a contact, moreover, is about to be established. But I must add that if it is one-sided it will bear no fruit.' Mann's insight is quite different from the occasional, critical remarks of Adrian and Serenus which reveal an abstract sympathy with the rising new world. For him, more and more, it is a perspective in which he sees the disintegrating bourgeois culture of the present, unable to find a solution in its own terms and poised on barbarism. Mann may not be able to give concrete embodiment to the 'great world' which the people (without quotation marks) are building. Nevertheless, it is sufficiently manifest everywhere for him to fulfil his tragedy of the declining world, to lay bare the 'small world' of 'pure spirit' for what it is—a deathly, devilish cell, something which its inhabitants as yet only dimly feel. In Shakespeare's greatest tragedies, *Hamlet, Lear*, the light of a new world gleams in the tragic darkness at the end. Who has the right to ask Shakespeare to provide an accurate social description of this new world? Does not the vision itself lend the light and shade of the tragedy their right proportions and emphases, social, intellectual, artistic?

Such is the sense and function of Adrian Leverkühn's last tragic insight: ' . . . instead of shrewdly concerning themselves with what is needful on earth that it may be better there, and discreetly doing it, that among men such order shall be stablished that again for the beautiful work living soil and true harmony be prepared, man playeth the truant and breaketh out in hellish drunkenness, so giveth his soul thereto and cometh among the carrion.'

We have quoted these words again because they give clear expression to what is new: the transformation of the real, the economic and social, basis of life as the first step towards the healing of mind and culture, thought and art. Thomas Mann's tragic hero has here found the way which leads to Marx. At least, in his last lucid words he has forsaken his own bedevilled path (the path of bourgeois culture and art) and described the new path which leads to a new 'great world', where a new, popular, great, never-again devilish art will be possible. The incomprehension of his friend and biographer provides a realistic frame to this perspective. Serenus regards his own loyalty to Adrian as an escape from Germany's fate. He views the defeat of fascism as a mockery of German history. Yet Adrian's perspective emerges logically from this tragedy and the tragedy of bourgeois art. It exists objectively. But the bourgeois intelligentsia has not yet accepted it as the way to light, out of the prison walls of their 'small world'.

The simple pronouncement of such a perspective is sufficient to relieve the tragedy of its despondency. Thomas Mann sets a full stop to a development of several centuries. But for this reason the epilogue is also a prologue. The tragedy remains, yet from the standpoint of humanity it is no more pessimistic than the great tragedies of Shakespeare.

1948.

The Playful Style

I

THIS essay must be fragmentary. Why? Because the work which determines its content, *The Confessions of Felix Krull, Confidence Man,* is still fragmentary despite its resumption. In aesthetics it is the end which has the last say. In life, on the other hand, we are almost always concerned with incomplete phenomena; even a person's death is only the end of his career in a very relative sense; his deeds and works continue to make themselves felt. Whatever sources we may find for our mistaken views of life, one thing is certain—these views will bear the *terminus a quo* imprint of the present.

Any view of literature, however, is ruled by a *terminus ad quem.* That is, the ultimate meaning of any character, the final look of any situation radiates out from the end, only the very end of course, the last decisive moment. The atmosphere which surrounds the characters and situations defines itself dynamically as a growth towards this end. It is this movement and its final chords which yield the atmosphere of a true work of art. Take Andrei Bolkonsky and Pierre Bezukhov in Tolstoy's *War and Peace.* The former, from his first proud appearance in the salon to his reconciling death after all disappointments, is enveloped in an air of unavoidable tragedy. The latter is constantly attended by an atmosphere of safety and trust; he is certain of a good outcome. Even when Bezukhov faces his French executioners this sense of security prevails.

Such moods do more than suggest the general shape of the story which is then fulfilled at the end, as if the conclusion were a reel to be unwound backwards. This unity of the story is rather the keynote to what is most specific and individual, determining the particular character both of the whole and the details. The irresistible charm of Goethe's *Egmont* is inseparable from its tragic end. Without this *hubris* which declares itself in Egmont's carefree, confident behaviour his charm would be no more than thoughtless folly.

Here then, as always when one has to do with real problems of form, one is dealing with a truth about life. If there is a consistent curve in a person's development from possibility to fulfilment then his life evinces a synthetic character from the outset. Novalis called this the unity of fortune and temperament, Goethe the deepest happiness of the personality—the bringing to ripeness of one's early tendencies. This phenomenon may sometimes receive a mystical or semi-mystical explanation. Yet it is an important fact of life, a very significant species of relationship between character and circumstances. It is also an extreme. In very many cases the core of personality is too weak to maintain a structural identity through a ceaseless continuity of change. Yet each person has a tendency in this direction, for good or ill, and most people would measure the value and depth of personality by this kind of constancy, this continuous development of inherent endowment; they would all desire it for themselves. Of course, the dialectical thesis of the unity of identity and nonidentity holds good here. The constant often undergo far more radical changes and upheavals than the inconstant. The point here is that a 'permanence in change'[1] is achieved: the core of personality keeps its balance through and by means of the most extreme metamorphoses.

Literature realizes this general belief and desire. The *terminus ad quem*, the determining function of the end is only a formal and compositional expression of an important problem of life.

[1] The title of a poem by Goethe.

The completion of a work, Stendhal's 'promesse de bonheur' always relates to those legitimate wishes of people which can only find a very partial and often distorted fulfilment in class society. A humanist protest against this situation is the theme of many writers, but in all good literature it lodges itself, too, in this problem of form.

Therefore, in judging any work which has not yet reached completion one should be sceptical towards oneself. This applies to my present unsystematic attempt to single out the central characteristics of *Krull*, awakened now out of decades of hibernation.

II

The style of the novel—to begin at a point not too far from our immediate problem—is determined by the character of the relations between being and consciousness, between man and environment. The more comprehensive and complete these relationships, the more realistic in scope and the more truthful in particulars, the more significant the novel. One must also look at these relationships historically. For not only is the environment of man, the economic structure of society caught in a ceaseless process of change, but each particular structure yields a changing and often quite different picture of the condition and consciousness of different classes. In *Resurrection* Tolstoy shows how various the relationships between being and consciousness can be by pointing out the attitudes to the state, its laws, lawcourts and prisons on the part of the ruling class, the defenceless victims and the revolutionaries. Thus the relations between being and consciousness, environment and man must widen into an intensive whole if any satisfying sense of completeness and finish is to be achieved.

To see this change in structure quite clearly, let us look at the difference between primitive accumulation and normally functioning capitalism. Marx says: 'Direct, non-economic force is still used, but only as an exception. In the general course of things the worker can be left to the "natural laws of production", that is to his dependence on capital which has sprung from the conditions of production themselves and which they have guaranteed and perpetuated. The rising bourgeoisie needs and uses state power to "regulate" wages (that is, to force them into the limits required for making surplus value), to increase the working day and to keep the worker himself at a normal level of dependence. This is an essential factor in so-called primitive accumulation.' This definition naturally describes only the two poles of a lengthy and extremely uneven process.

The great novels of the early bourgeois period like *Moll Flanders, Gil Blas* and in a certain sense *Tom Jones* portray bourgeois society in its emergence, with all its gaps and fissures bringing luck or ruin, with all its brutal violence and corrupt impotence. But in the end energy and resourcefulness triumph. With Balzac the gaps are sealed, the immanent, economic laws of capitalism all-powerful. The cultural ambitions of men, their feelings and thoughts, their giftedness and responsiveness turn into commodities just like the technical instruments which propagate and communicate them—the printing-press and the newspapers. Nevertheless, the rearguard battle which is fought here still retains the form of a real struggle, although there can no longer be any doubt about its outcome. Flaubert, however, describes a world in which these struggles are resolved. In *Madame Bovary* the social environment has reached a maximum of density. The relations of people to this environment, therefore, are reduced to impotent dreaming and passive capitulation or reluctant, merely outward, accommodation. This interplay is quite different for the same period in Russia. In my Pushkin study I showed how the chain of revolutionary attempts, the unbroken continuity of a revolutionary outlook affected literature and its portrayal of man and his environment. Here, therefore, there are always ways out of the 'density' of this fast-becoming capitalist country, even if they are mostly tragic. If one mentally contrasts Anna Karenina with Emma Bovary, Andrei Bolkonsky with Frédéric Moreau the difference is evident.

Imperialism sharpens the objective and the subjective antagonisms. Objectively, we can see both an increase in the surrounding 'density', the spread of the power of monopoly capital to all spheres of life, the control of the slightest stirrings of life by fascism, etc., and the reappearance of the gaps, the sudden break in continuity as a result of the frequent shocks to the whole structure of society administered by the world crises and world wars, the revolutions and counter-revolutions. Yet, in the main, all this is reflected in a consciousness which itself is a victim of imperialism, which suffers simultaneously from a false objectivism and a false subjectivism and hence doubly distorts reality. Men sense the pressure, the constraint of the social categories on their personal lives more painfully than in any previous social order. At the same time, the moral precepts which transmit this pressure appear far less self-evident, far less binding than in earlier societies. The loneliness of artists, their abandonment to themselves, which this situation produces, is only aggravated and deepened by a subjectivist ideology.

Hence Gotfried Benn wrote some decades ago: ' . . . In Europe between 1910 and 1925 there was no other style but the anti-naturalist. There was no reality either, at most there were its masks. Reality, that was a capitalist concept. . . . The mind had no reality.' Hence Ernst Bloch says of the reality of his day, it was a 'perfect non-world, anti-world or world of ruins in a *grandbourgeois* vacuum'. What does this unanimously intoned 'no reality' mean, when used by authors so entirely opposed to one another in outlook? Above all what does it mean to the writer? Ernst Bloch's answer is vivid and right: 'Writers of significance can no longer find their way into their material except by smashing it. The prevailing world no longer offers them a representable illusion which may be fashioned into a story, but just emptiness and inside this some mixable rubble.'

It is not difficult to elicit the objective situation from such subjective testimonies. Men in the imperialist age have lost all perspective both as regards society and their own existence. But with perspective they also lose their ability to distinguish between essence and appearance; the objective nature of social determinism becomes unrecognizable. If for artistic reasons this determinism must be constructed or reconstructed, caprice and distortion inevitably step in. But no real picture of reality is possible without a perspective, even a negative one as in *L'Education Sentimentale*. In this ruined world of vanished realities, this Golgotha of lost illusions the individual turns tragi-comic autocrat and governs according to fancy. What appear to be disconnected pieces of reality he arranges as he pleases, now adjacently, now far apart; from these isolated and, in their isolation, meaningless fragments of reality he patches together his dadaist or surrealist 'compositions'. The loss of perspective and essence creates the illusion of a reality destroyed and the limitless dominion of subjectivity—a subjectivity with a bad conscience, for it can never rid itself of the fear that the least contact with objective reality will collapse such intellectual and emotional card-houses.

Can any kind of realism emerge from such inflated subjectivity? Yes and no. No, if this subjectivity aims at a comprehensive picture of the world by forcefully adapting the determinants of objective reality to itself. Yes, in marginal cases, if for instance a conscious effort is made so to restrict the compass of reality, and the radius of its inner determinants, that the world which is adapted to the subject can be presented with realist method and intention. In significant cases where this has succeeded the problem has been a purely moral one of personal endurance in face of *nature*. If social relationships had been allowed to enter, even on the horizon, the conflicts issuing from them would have been doomed from the outset, given this particular attitude and method. It is no doubt thought and said that moral problems acquire a 'cosmic' depth in this way. In reality the world presented shrinks to the relationship of the isolated individual to certain isolated natural forces. This is how it was with Joseph Conrad's *Typhoon*. So, too, with Hemingway's *The Old Man and the Sea*, where the human relations are still further reduced.

In both cases the writer has the artistic good sense to contain his theme—of isolated, purely personal endurance in face of natural forces—within the form of the *novella*.[1] The novels of Conrad and Hemingway give clear enough indication of the modern predicament. This reposes, as a result of the inevitable disappearance of social relations between men, upon an impoverishment of man's relationship to himself. Wherever such gaps are filled in with substitutes, even highly gifted authors must approach mere belletrism. Only now and again do we meet the paradoxical case of a writer who succeeds in expanding his *novella* into a real novel, as in Conrad's extremely interesting *Lord Jim*. Here is not the place for a detailed analysis of this problem; we will content ourselves with saying that it always involves a certain 'worldlessness' in the particular objective reality selected.

Thomas Mann establishes this dissolution perceptively in Joyce. His only mistake is to connect these tendencies with his own. In *The Genesis of a Novel* he quotes with approval an interpreter of Joyce who says of *Ulysses* it is a novel to end all novels. And commenting on a similar statement of T. S. Eliot's, Mann asks 'whether in the field of the novel, nowadays the only thing that counted was what was no longer a novel'; and he thinks this applies equally to *The Magic Mountain*, *Joseph* and *Doctor Faustus*.

No doubt there are plenty of formal resemblances. It suffices if I recall the doubling of time in *Faustus*. However, this apparent affinity arises only from the material, the choice of theme, not from the method. Thomas Mann sets himself the legitimate and central task of an imaginative historian of our time—to

---

[1] The German word is *Novelle* which I have used whenever it has applied to German literature, where it has a special and local meaning. *Novella* here simply means long short-story.

portray the subjectivity of bourgeois man in the imperialist period, man without perspective in real interaction with his environment. If he wishes to do justice to his theme, then of course he must present his characters, their relations with the world in a manner typical of our time. That is, he gives us a picture of similar men and fates as we find in the works of Joyce, Hemingway, Gide, etc. The social tendencies which warp and distort the personality of the characters and their relationship to reality he makes just as visible as these his well-known contemporaries.

But despite the similarity of theme the differences in artistic outlook and hence in form are more important. First, the modernists write with no sort of perspective on the future of mankind. Thomas Mann has a perspective: that socialism is unavoidable if (which he does not believe) the human race is not to be swallowed up in barbarism. True, this is an abstract perspective which on the one hand says little or nothing about the nature of socialism and on the other leaves undiscussed the problems of transition from present-day society to a future one. In Mann's artistic world as a result there can be no manifestation of this transition in human terms. Nevertheless, the sheer existence of a perspective creates conditions and possibilities for treating the present which would be absent with no perspective at all. Secondly, then, if Thomas Mann takes the subjectivism of the imperialist period as a theme which he feels to be both typical and near to him, he handles it as a *theme,* never as a *principle.* Modern subjectivity occupies a central place in his work, but it is shown *as* subjectivity. It is confronted by an outer world which moves according to independent, objective laws and with which it is continually forced into contact; it is set in a historically appropriate milieu which gives it scope to develop. The structural categories of the outside world are not determined by the subjectivity, but on the contrary determine it, its nature, growth, development. In a word, Thomas Mann does what his contemporaries fail to do: he allocates modern subjectivity its proper place in his picture of present-day society.

If two people do the same thing, it does not mean that the thing is the same. Virginia Woolf's use of a double time dissolves continuity and connection. In Thomas Mann's hands it strengthens the sense of social reality. The time in which Serenus Zeitblom writes his biography in Dr. *Faustus* emphasizes the social consequences of Adrian Leverkühn's life and work. It underlines in a very simple way the essential bond between the hero and a Germany becoming fascist, though Leverkühn himself is not aware of it and, were he, would repudiate the idea with angry disdain.

The time problem is, of course, not the only one where an apparent similarity conceals an antithesis. This was only just one example. Let us quote another. André Gide in his Dostoyevsky study mentions certain paradoxes in Blake (which he re-interprets in a modern Gidean sense) and adds: 'One creates bad literature with beautiful feelings' and: 'No work of art is possible without the help of the devil.' The devilish theme then is made into a necessary principle of all artistic creation. The situation appears similarly to Leverkühn in Mann's *Faustus*. But, and this is the point, to Leverkühn (and Gide), not to Thomas Mann. Mann indeed uses his devil very ironically to point out the difference to Leverkühn—a historical difference, a situation which did not exist for Goethe and his times but does for the age of imperialism: 'That is it,' says the devil here, 'you do not think of the passage of time, you do not think historically, when you complain that such and such a one could have it "wholly", joys and pains endlessly, without the hour-glass being set for him, the reckoning finally made. What he in his classical decades could have without us, certainly, that nowadays, we alone have to offer.' Thus what for Gide, whom we take only as an example, is a matter of principle is simply a theme in Mann.

The same is demonstrable for all the supposed similarities between Thomas Mann and the decadent *avant-garde*. The meeting-point is only in the theme, the material; it occurs stylistically only insofar as the theme requires illustration. Where the essential problems of form are concerned the contact is at a minimum, present only when similar manifestations require similar techniques. Mann has certainly 'modernized' his style ever since *Buddenbrooks*, but not in order to link himself with the dissolution of the novel as a form. On the contrary he continues the best traditions of the realist novel, but in the conditions of bourgeois society of the imperialist period in which content and form have inevitably changed. It is because Thomas Mann has got so to the core of his epoch that he can so self-deceivingly align himself with those whose only skill lies in snapshot *montage* or stylized distortion of the immediate surface. The fact that with all his contemporaneity he remains a preserver of the best epic traditions has been often attested by his modernist critics who accuse him of 'bourgeois cultivation' and would make of him a poet of 'security'. One needs to separate out both these extremes in order to discover the real problems of style in Mann's writing.

The basic tendency is visible from the outset, but it grows in clarity and intricacy. Everyone knows Mann's stylistic manner: irony, self-irony, humour, the music of reservation. Here too his link with the older literature is evident; it suffices to mention Fontane. However, Mann's style is not to be deduced from stylistic influences, even at the beginning of his career; it grows organically out of the social being of his epoch, out of contemporary moods and problems. In short, it is a question of the discrepancy between a subjective reflection of reality (with which Mann's specifically moral problems are concerned—self-control, disintegration and their contradictory unity) and the actual, objective world itself. Therefore the modernist denial of objective reality makes no sense in Mann's world.

The discrepancies of life may have a tragic or comic issue; Thomas Mann follows Socrates' demand in the *Symposium* that the same poet should write tragedies and comedies. Of course, to combine the tragic and the comic is to make them relative. This was first formulated as a historical concept by Karl Marx. But since Thomas Mann is treating the tragic and comic collisions of his own epoch (even where his immediate theme is the Joseph legend), this historical relativity is translated into a typology for the present. The stress is laid on the transitions from the tragic to the comic and *vice versa*; what historically is not adjacent appears morally so, as a moral hierarchy of possible responses to contemporary problems.

Thomas Mann achieved his sense of perspective after difficult struggles with himself, overcoming very deep-rooted illusions. Yet in a negative way this perspective was present from the outset, manifesting itself as an ingrained scepticism towards contemporary bourgeois society. The fact that for a long time neither Mann nor his readers were able to recognize the true intent of this scepticism does not alter its objective existence which is now quite clear.

It was a consequence of this scepticism in the young Thomas Mann that tragedy would always appear grotesque; so with Thomas Buddenbrook, so more markedly with Gustav von Aschenbach. In turn this meant that the realism was always tinged with fantasy. For underlying the realistic-fantastic *grotesquerie* were the opposites of appearance and essence, consciousness and reality, which had been imaginatively sharpened. The dominant *motif* in this period was, typically, the ironic death. In the case of both Thomas Buddenbrook and Gustav von Aschenbach death in its degrading forms seems to defy all the hero has stood for, all his noble stoicism. Yet life and death, the inner world and the outer are connected (and here we can see the philosophic basis of Mann's irony and self-irony). The grotesque end of Thomas Buddenbrook and Gustav von Aschenbach, characters who mean a lot to their author, forms their essential epitaph. Where the tragedy is less tense the grotesque has no need to appear in the guise of death. Yet even as comedy it is never 'pure'; it never detaches itself from the personal problems of the young Mann, which were very serious for him at the time—take Tonio Kröger's near-arrest or Detlev Spinell's great showdown with

Klöterjahn. An ironic light-fantastic style springs up out of these attitudes, reaching an early climax in the short-story *The Wardrobe*.

The gradual but increasingly clear transition of Mann's irony and self-irony into the playful is determined by two components. On the one hand, the consciousness of his most important characters recedes ever more distantly from objective reality; on the other, reality asserts its supremacy over all kinds of false consciousness ever more vigorously. For this reason Mann's playfulness never dissolves objective reality, but on the contrary underlines its inevitable and natural triumph. The greater the discrepancy between being and consciousness, the more grotesque and degrading must the defeat of subjectivity be. In terms of form the playful is a fantastic to-and-fro between temporary lodgements of false consciousness and the 'treachery' with which objectivity tolerates, indeed fosters such illusions. The false consciousness is lulled in its illusion, vaguely aware that it may not last, until it is undeceived finally by some grotesque-comic or tragi-comic catastrophe.

This is what determines the atmosphere of *Royal Highness*. Prince Albrecht is quite aware of the *vaudeville* he is forced to play and the paralysing effect it has on human enterprise and activity. He is relatively well aware of the meaninglessness of his own social existence. Yet such is the nature and power of this existence that he is unable to make the slightest effort to leave it. The see-saw between insight and illusion is no less humorous and playful in the case of Prince Klaus Heinrich and his 'high calling'; even his genuine love is rent by this irony. The more serious intent of the playful soon makes itself felt in Mann's work. He places his characters in an extremely original and specific world where such aberrations of consciousness may achieve pure expression. The playfulness of the plot and the irony of the narrative have the function of fostering this pure culture to an extreme and at the same time of making it collide with true, socially typical reality.

The Magic Mountain takes this a step forward. It marks a turning-point in Mann's work, in that the negative scepticism of the pre-war period here begins to crystallize out as a perspective of development. The discrepancies of the early Mann may appear more extreme, the surface style show more affinity with modernism; but at the same time the essential differences have taken firm root. The ironic see-saw moves more variously, but it comes down more decisively on the side of objective reality. This occurs on three planes: first, the historically inevitable false consciousness; second, its corresponding environment, the isolated magic mountain; third, actual reality which constantly unmasks the unreality, the deception of the two former planes. The greater the distances between the planes, the more marked the irony and self-irony. The distance, of course, may appear both directly and indirectly. Where it seems to disappear completely, as in the quagmire atmosphere towards the end of *The Magic Mountain*, its apparent absence only emphasizes its real presence and invisible operativeness in every essential human question. It is a way, quite new, of presenting the conflicts of present-day consciousness against the background of an invisible reality. The antithesis to modernism is obvious; the latter is only able to use the first of Mann's three components.

It is impossible to give even the merest sketch of all these relationships; we must content ourselves with a few indications. Without question the *Joseph* novels mark the apex of this style. The immediate reality here is mythical. But the outlook which created Mann's three components also strengthened his sense of perspective. Hence the play, the ironic and self-ironic see-saw between the three components acquires a new and original character. The mythical world of the novels has to do service for both reality-components: the illusory one in which the consciousness makes its home and the actual which ironically deflates it. What is new in the form of the *Joseph* novels is that the narrative has to perform both these functions, which of course increases the play, the irony and self-irony. A way then must be found of presenting reality which can make what is self-created appear credible and acceptable and yet at the same time nullify and destroy it. The see-saw of the earlier novels between two realities becomes purely inward here, an immanent movement within the same reality, between its two poles—stylistically a step towards modernism, but again in the deeper sense of form its strict opposite. Modernism is well-versed in conjuring with extremes, but their trajectory lies between a false consciousness (unrecognized as such) and its 'special' reality; subjectivism then is the ruling principle for both outlook and method. In Thomas Mann, however, the imagined reality oscillates with the real (objective) one and the latter is always victorious, even where, as here, both realities appear united in the myth. The fact that such deflation here has the dual function of destroying and preserving (the writer, that is, upholds his fictions *as* fictions) cannot alter this antithesis.

Thomas Mann's exploration of the mythical depths of middle-Eastern folklore therefore did not weaken the supremacy of the real over the imagined, but on the contrary strengthened it. His sense of perspective has never emerged so clearly as in the final novel *Joseph the Provider*. And this is important for all the works written during and after the cycle. We shall pick out only one of the many new *motifs*. Thomas Mann begins (admittedly in secondary works) to allot a decisive role to the purely physical basis of life and consciousness, to make biological reality a potent factor of personality. Of course, ever since *Little Herr Friedemann* the physical make-up of his characters had been important for what happened to them. But there is a qualitative difference between what is a point of departure, the outward form of a catastrophe and the process which determines the heart of a collision as in the later works *The Transposed Heads* and *The Black Swan*. *The Transposed Heads* like *The Holy Sinner* is set in a fantastic 'special' world and obedient to its laws, while *The Black Swan* is a direct realist work about the present. Yet the character of the two tales is essentially similar.

In every case the imaginatively real is the truly real, simply as the force that decides. But it is never a brute, fatalistic force, not even in its biological form. Obviously, the false consciousness is being tested here against the fundamental conditions of life and hence must rightly come to grief. But a subtle dialectic intervenes. On the one hand the false consciousness is subjectively justified because reality itself of necessity creates it; on the other Thomas Mann, like Shakespeare or Balzac, knows that even the falsest consciousness is not without its grain of truth and that it is impossible to live with a completely false consciousness. This (admittedly very relative) subjective justification applies not just to the genesis of passions. It may, as at the end of *The Holy Sinner*, triumph as the final victory of will-power and resourcefulness; or, as in *The Black Swan*, achieve a tragi-ironic reconciliation with fate, where the ill and dying mother, deceived and misled by her own physical condition, is yet more truly alive, essentially younger than her 'healthy' daughter (whose physical dialectics and fate we cannot go into here).

The irony is deeper here, the play intensified. In *The Black Swan* modern abstract painting is deftly refuted by casually linking it with the biological tragedy of the intelligent daughter. Freud's Oedipus complex is reduced to absurdity in *The Holy Sinner* by the resourcefulness and essentially healthy and worldly morality of the hero. As in the tragic case of Leverkühn with Nietzsche, so here with Freud, Mann, the imaginative writer, thinks so much more rightly and healthily than Mann, the idea-spinning essayist. For him, the son of a divided and deeply problematic period and class the play of irony and self-irony is an important means for overcoming artistically what is necessarily beyond him personally and intellectually. Writers of more fortunate, less divided times and classes, like Balzac for example, throw together the intellectually wrong and the artistically right in crude and stark opposition, seeking truth, to use Marx's words, 'in the very dungheap of contradictions'. Mann's ideological aims then are essentially similar to the older realists; only his means differ because of the different times. On the other hand his resemblance to contemporary modernists in matters of technique conceals the world of a difference in artistic purpose and outlook.

Once again the problem of perspective is decisive. Its positive turn is illustrated in Joseph's development where the activity that fulfils him personally also contributes to the well-being of his fellow men, and where such activity has become a natural mode of conduct. In the case of Adrian Leverkühn the perspective appears in his belated recognition of the only right path: ' . . . instead of shrewdly concerning themselves with what is needful upon earth that it may be better there, and discreetly doing it, that among men such order shall be stablished that again for the beautiful work living soil and true harmony be prepared, man playeth truant and breaketh out in hellish drunkenness; so giveth his soul thereto and cometh among the carrion.'

Such moments of consciousness are only the clearest manifestations of the constituent principle which underlies Mann's picture of the world in all his later works. The insight and wisdom, that Mann achieves, determines—positively and negatively—the fate of each of his characters. They are not lonely 'heroes' who discover some abstract-moral position for themselves alone, as in Conrad or Hemingway. They seek their way in society, in common with others, losing it, partially and totally, or finding it with relative success. From now on action, activity is Mann's guide to characterization. And this is the sense of the biological playful in works like The Holy Sinner and The Black Swan.

This then is the background to Mann's playful phantasy. Hence it differs sharply from all previous and apparently similar forms. Hoffmann, for example, a contemporary of dying feudalism and early, abortive petty bourgeois capitalism in Germany, makes the most typical figures of this transition appear as ghosts. The central question of his style then is the extent to which these ghosts can credibly appear alongside the actual characters and their human environment. Thus in identifying dissimilars and dissolving identifications the two writers have in fact an opposite aim. A somewhat closer resemblance may be found in Gottfried Keller and the ironic phantasy of a story like *Spiegel the Kitten*. Here the phantasy cloaks real connections in a fairytale, rainbow-coloured, improbably genine world, the irony playing on the contrasts between illusion, self-deception and truth. Such *motifs* predominate in Mann, too, but they do not have that absoluteness that they do in Keller, their effect is only ultimate. And this shift in proportion is so marked that it produces quite new qualities in content and form. This ultimate effect comes over in the extremely complex interplay of subjective and objective forces, inevitable deceptions, self-deceptions, error and truth.

It is this intricate criss-crossing of forces which forms Mann's picture of our time. The phantasy brings out the essential by *détour*; the playful is the motor which intensifies and relaxes, which stresses and refrains so that in each individual case the specific proportion of error and truth is disclosed. This is why the irony and self-irony are so necessary both in the case of a realistically portrayed condition of isolation in the present and of a present-day content transposed into the mythical, fantastic past. The playful is always a vehicle of truth and reality in the end. These complex motions create a wide artistic field and an extraordinary variety of themes and forms. Outwardly their selectness and singularity constantly border on mannerism, but so strong is the pressure that makes for truth and reality, that seeks out the perspective of our lives, so concrete is the picture that emerges from all these tendencies that mannerism is avoided and transcended.

This style is deeply realistic for all the apparently unrealistic ingredients which we have described. The abstract character of his socialist perspective separates Mann's work from socialist realism, but makes it the highest and so far last great expression of bourgeois, critical realism today. It is a bourgeois world, seen by a bourgeois, but by one who looks with an unprejudiced eye and who, in his judgment of the present, his grasp of its essential character and in his understanding of the future, transcends his own class limitations.

III

The Confessions of Felix Krull, Confidence Man were put to one side in favour of *Death in Venice* and for decades remained a fragment. On the completion of *Joseph and His Brethren* the manuscript was resumed and for a very short time competed with *Dr. Faustus*. In his diary, after having re-read the old sketches, Thomas Mann compared and contrasted the two themes, thus: '... insight into the inner kinship of the Faust subject with this one (the motif of loneliness, in the one case mystic and tragic, in the other humorous and roguish); nevertheless my feeling is that the Faust, if I am capable of shaping it, is more appropriate for me today, more topical, more urgent....' Therewith, in a nutshell, Thomas Mann fixed the position of *Krull* in his life's work.

He also adds a few other important remarks on the *Krull* fragment. He mentions in his diary a conversation with his wife about the fragment and the desire of friends that he should continue it. He comments: 'The idea is not altogether alien to me, but I had considered the book, which springs from a period when the artist-bourgeois problem was my most dominant concern, superannuated and outmoded by the *Joseph*!' The reference is extremely illuminating; it embraces the impression Mann retained of his *Krull* plan and its connection with his early work together with his realization of having moved away from this sphere in the *Joseph* novels.

The move beyond the artist-bourgeois problem was also its generalization. In a previous study I described this combination of continuation and departure by saying that the mental and moral problem of *Tonio Kröger* had been resumed, but that it was no longer connected with the life of the artist. What had been the central question for the young Thomas Mann had been socially generalized; the simple antithesis of artist and bourgeois had been brought into the larger context of social practice as a whole. There is a lot to be said then for Mann's description of the Joseph cycle as a shuffling-off of his own early problems. Nevertheless, I do not think that the objective pattern of Mann's writing is quite identical with this impression. I have also tried to show previously that *Death in Venice*, though rooted in the artist-bourgeois conflict, nevertheless, at least partially, moves or certainly points the way beyond it. Thomas Mann himself refers to this argument and points out the inner relationship 'between the Venetian *Novelle* and *Faustus*'.

The connection, I think, is threefold. First, the problem of the artist (classically portrayed in *Tonio Kröger*) immediately gives rise to the problem of art as such. Secondly, the relationship to the present, the imperialist period, becomes altogether richer and more articulated. The menace of the mental underworld assumes shape here for the first time, which was completely lacking in the first artist stories. Thirdly, and again for the first time in Thomas Mann, artistic activity is judged as a form of social action. Before, it was merely a question of the artist's loneliness in bourgeois life and his withdrawal from it. *Death in Venice* pushes this tendency to its extreme, but by doing so shows how inevitably paradoxical is the social function of art in bourgeois society; and this apart from anything else makes the story an early prelude to *Dr. Faustus*. The connections then are varied and complex—but, seen in this light, is Mann's first impression that the problems of this transition had been outdated by the *Joseph* novels object-ively valid?

I do not think so. On the contrary, I do not consider it at all an accident that the *Krull* plan did not become relevant again until after the *Joseph* novels, nor do I believe that this is to be explained simply (or even mainly) by the parallel with *Faustus* suggested above. I think Krull is essentially a complement, an ironic counterpart to Joseph.

This assertion needs a little more argument. In the *Joseph* novels Thomas Mann took up and treated (adapting theme and form to his own day) one of the chief problems of the classical period, namely the self-enjoyment of personality. In the early period of bourgeois literature this question had not yet separated itself out. Self-enjoyment of personality appeared as the natural consequence, the inevitable by-product of a successfully waged struggle in life; it acquired a slightly more independent emphasis as a humanist, this-worldly polemic against a medieval or puritanical asceticism. In the late bourgeois period any such self-enjoyment has become an unattainable goal. In Tolstoy, especially, one can observe how many of the supposedly religious elements in his major works derive from this problem. Tolstoy grasps very precisely the moral antinomy of bourgeois society: on the one hand pleasure realized is the mark of a thoroughly inferior egoist; not only has it an unworthy object, but its subjective manifestation is humanly degrading. On the other hand the morally pure and genuine people in the society, that Tolstoy knows and describes, can find satisfaction neither subjectively nor objectively, neither in themselves nor in their activity; decency inevitably turns into self-tormenting asceticism. Hence as consolation on the horizon there appears the specifically Tolstoyan religious experience, Konstantin Levin's, for example. But Levin's creator, a brilliant and intelligent observer of his time, cannot go on for long with such illusions, certainly not as a writer. Rather he must close every imaginary route out of the dilemma with bitter, self-critical irony. Between these two historical poles lies the brief interlude of German classicism; in particular *Wilhelm Meister's Apprenticeship* where the interim Utopia achieves its purest form.

No detailed discussion is needed to see that Mann's early work is determined by the Tolstoyan antinomy, though without Tolstoy's illusions about a religious way-out. The inner-worldly asceticism, the rejection of all immediate forms of egoism is perhaps more aggressive and negative in the young Mann than in Tolstoy himself. This shows itself not only in the problem of profession and code of conduct, which I have repeatedly analysed, but in the complete emptiness of Thomas Buddenbrook's enjoyment of life and self. This is particularly true of the main character in the story *The Bajazzo*. Here the type caricatures himself with self-knowledge. 'There is,' he says, summing up his own life, 'only one kind of unhappiness—to lose pleasure in oneself. No longer to please oneself, that is unhappiness; yes, I have always known that well. All else is play and embroidery upon life; in any other kind of suffering one can still remain altogether satisfied with oneself, cut a fine figure in one's own eyes. Only discord with yourself, loss of self-approval in your suffering, the conflicts which vanity imposes, only these can render you a wretched and repulsive spectacle.' At the other end of the pole—the dilemma of composure, which, at this stage of Mann's development, includes, and also constrains, the artist-bourgeois problem. Loss of composure signifies the total collapse of a way of life, the loss of personality and the possibility of wholehearted self-enjoyment. But this is to shift the problem on to an (admittedly not unimportant) sidetrack. Thomas Mann's main argument neighbours on certain ironic asides of late Goethe. Mephistopheles, for instance, says of the young Emperor:

> Denn jung ward ihm der Thron zu Teil,
> Und ihm beliebt' es, falsch zu schliessen:
> Es könne wohl zusammengehn,
> Und sei recht wünschenswert und schön,
> Regieren und zugleich geniessen.

> For he was crowned while yet a youth,
> And liked to draw the false conclusion:
> That it's desirable and fine,
> And practicable to combine,
> Kingship and pleasure in collusion.

In Goethe the breakdown is more outward, in early Mann more inward.

The first sketch of *Krull* (as we have shown for *Death in Venice*) immediately points to a more general statement. The discontinuation of *Krull* may be explained by this new and not entirely clear situation. The tragi-comic and grotesque end of Gustav von Aschenbach gives an answer to the problems that arise here, but in the form of a *Novelle*, concentrated, intensive, ungeneralized therefore, although pointing prophetically ahead. With the artistic equipment of the time it was impossible to cope with the Krull type who required an extensive humorous treatment, hence a capacious real world. It was no accident, therefore, that the work stopped short on the threshold of Krull's entry into life proper. Mann could embrace in his poetic vision the purely mental components of Krull; but the representation of the world, interacting with which these social-moral seeds grew to fruition, had to wait for a later period in his development. In this light *Death in Venice* also acquires a new aspect in the progress of Mann's work. Aschenbach's story already points to the problems of action in our time. Yet (and this is in full accord with the self-contained form of the *Novelle*) it indicates more the social, psychological and moral premises and consequences than action itself.

Both works then (whether finished or fragmentary) anticipate later tendencies, give intimations of that great crossroads with which the First World War was to confront Thomas Mann and so many others. The process itself cannot even be sketched out here. Let it be said simply that the intimations embraced not only the problems of *Reflections of an Unpolitical Man*, but also the path which Thomas Mann would take beyond these problems after the end of the war. I have also discussed the inner contradictions of the last work in previous studies. Here suffice it that from the standpoint of Mann's career it constituted a *reculer pour mieux sauter*.

Again we can do no more than touch upon the works which followed. *The Magic Mountain* is an epic of the premises of social action in the world of today. Castorp's adventure encompasses in a true epic whole the content and form of the choice which must precede all action. The interlude of *Disorder and Early Sorrow* voices in a lyrical confessional tone, underscored therefore by self-irony and reservation, the fears that the new tasks inspire. In *Mario and the Magician*, on the other hand, we have for the first time in Mann, in the person of Cipolla, the psychology and behaviour of a pronounced reactionary in action (Naphta had only provided the ideological basis and moral temptations). Whenever Thomas Mann had shown people before who had set back his humanist line (for instance, the Hagenströms in *Buddenbrooks*), they did so purely from the outside, chronicle-wise as it were. This too has deeper causes than the stylistic principles themselves. The social-critical basis of *Buddenbrooks* was still a romantic anti-capitalism. The Hagenströms therefore represented (in a way Mann could not disentangle at the time) both economic progress and human and cultural regression. What is reactionary, too, only becomes clear to Thomas Mann, only receives a rational imaginative analysis when his social perspective in relation to the future of the bourgeoisie has become clear. And only in this context can the opposition and struggle between reaction and people achieve expression. Mario's hypnotic seduction by Cipolla, his awakening from the demagogic stupor, his revenge on the seducer—this is Mann's first political literary work. It provides concept and image for Mann's large canvases of human action in the social world.

Tantae molis erat . . . to trace the ideological basis of the *Joseph* novels. But once again we must limit ourselves to a few indications to shed just a little more light on our specific problem. The central question of the cycle is the education of Joseph from the dreamy, self-regarding youth to a mature, active member of society; who by learning the real nature of the world and by usefully and productively acting within it can achieve genuine self-enjoyment on a higher level.

As we have already remarked here, and in more detail elsewhere, art considered as activity in society is at the core of

Faustus. Adrian Leverkühn himself scorns pleasure more fiercely than Tonio Kröger and Gustav von Aschenbach; he is more proudly self-sufficient than they. Yet the nub of the story is no longer the subjective attitude of the artist, nor even its inner dialectic, as in the case of Aschenbach, but the social function of artistic activity, the emergence of artistic styles from and their re-entry into society. Hence Leverkühn's repudiation of personal pleasure acquires a quite new and more comprehensive meaning. In this respect, too, his great intellectual duel with the devil is but the culmination of his mode of life and outlook; of his conviction that no pure pleasure can be gained from art either by the creator or the recipient, that art, if it is really honest and contemporary, can only be parodistic; that it requires an inner coldness, the inebriate and ecstatic coldness of the inhuman and anti-human. The sincere Adrian Leverkühn is a tragic victim, but this cannot alter the objective character of his development, which leads to fascism as inevitably as the society whose product he is.

The enjoyment of personality in the *Joseph* novels is the positive counterpart to the devilish asceticism of the *Faustus* tragedy. Both novels belong to the intellectual and moral struggle against Hitlerism; Leverkühn as the type of the victim, Joseph as his counter-type. It is certainly no accident that in this struggle the most important German anti-fascists created challenging, positive characters of this kind: Heinrich Mann in *Henri Quatre*, Thomas Mann in *Joseph* (and in the Goethe of *Lotte in Weimar* which we shall not discuss in order not to complicate matters unnecessarily).

The struggle begins some time before fascism itself, as a struggle against imperialism; not only against its political and social, but also its inner, anti-human forces; for example in the work of Anatole France and Romain Rolland. While this countermovement sees a perspective ahead its imaginative task must be to present man of the imperialist period, darkly-despairing or cynically resigned, with a positive, alternative image. The problem of pleasure immediately becomes relevant again, for as soon as it is possible to believe in a renewed, regenerated human society, in which one may play a meaningful and rational part, self-enjoyment is the spontaneous mental reflex. The perspective of regeneration is indispensable. Without such an outlook there can only be self-satisfied, egoistic, narrow-minded or cynical reconciliation with the society of the present. Yet such a perspective is bound to be somewhat Utopian, whether one looks to a democratic renewal of bourgeois society or to socialism for saving mankind. The new man created in this perspective will not find a natural home in the present; he is the citizen of a new society, one that is to come. (This dilemma, of course, only faces bourgeois realism; a socialist realist may very well portray transitional figures, fighters for change. That critical realism must come to grief in this question is proved most clearly by Jacques Thibault's fate at the end of Roger Martin du Gard's ambitious and hitherto outstanding cycle of novels.)

All this needed saying so that we should be able to appreciate the resumed *Krull*, written now from a superior vantage-point, as the satyr-piece to the two great works of Mann's maturity, but more to *Joseph* than to *Faustus*. This broad and far-flung horizon to *Krull* is surely the main reason why the story was put aside at the time and has only been resumed after decades.

It is striking how many small, large, secondary and important features in the original *Krull* point ironic parallels to the character of Joseph. Here one can see clearly with how sure a touch and many-sided an energy Thomas Mann seizes reality in his poetic vision; how he is already able to fix in a single stage the essential pattern of meanings and symbols before their intellectual content has properly matured. Take, for instance, the singular beauty of the two characters, in particular their golden-brown skins. Take (to touch on their psychology) the ecstatic convulsions. Think of their equal adaptability in whatever occupation they are called to—pleasant, unpleasant, diverting or tedious; their skill at getting inside another's mind and flattering him accordingly whenever they so wish. In these and similar traits there is an inseparable mixture of seriousness and play. The behaviour of both veers ironically between a consciously conducted comedy, relying on the utmost application, on a genuine 'play' with the psyche of one's partner, on a fine adjudgment of his reactions, between this and a conscious aloofness, a purposeful pursuit of a fixed aim. In both cases self-delight is more than an affirmative reflex or subsequent recollection, it consciously accompanies and encourages action. This is what gives to many of their scenes that light-handed magic and depth. In the old *Krull* fragment this tendency reaches its peak in the recruiting scene where Krull in a brilliant piece of play-acting convinces everyone of his permanent unfitness for military service, leaving himself free to follow his own path as a confidence-trickster.

Naturally, these similar qualities are differently proportioned and weighted. Otherwise, how could Joseph become the 'provider' of a large nation, while Krull's talents go no further than individual confidence tricks? However, one must not forget that for all Joseph's developmental abilities and prowess, for all his innate seriousness he is not averse from confidence tricking and deception, particularly as the young Joseph. When, for instance, having received Rachel's coat from his father, Joseph is accused in this sense by Rueben, the criticism (whatever the envy or resentment that goes with it) is justified. Reuben charges Joseph with having deliberately let his father win in the game of stones in order to mend his temper; of having talked him out of the coat of many colours against his will: 'Ah, so, thou reminded him and begged him for it. He gave it thee against his will, tempted by thine. Knowest thou that it is against God to misuse the power that is given thee so that he willeth unjustly and doth what he regretteth?' In the language of the myth this is a not ungrounded accusation of confidence tricking.

Finally, let me briefly mention the parallel of the 'pits'. In Joseph's life there are two main turning-points in which 'the pit' figures as a symbol of fall and resurrection, namely his clash with his brothers and then with Potiphar and his wife. The *Krull* fragment even in its original version clearly indicates that such 'pits', in the prosaic modern form of a prison, play their part in Krull's career. But in this question, despite the publication of the first part of the memoirs, we may only register the fact as such. Causes and consequences of Krull's 'pit' are still to be shown. Nevertheless, this is a decisive question for both works. In the *Joseph* novels the 'pit' is much more than an outward solution of collisions. It twice, each time more intensely, releases a cathartic crisis in Joseph, which is brought on by the most dangerous side of his self-enjoyment—the conviction that 'everyone loves him more than they do themselves'. (I have indicated the connection between this mental trait and the German tragedy elsewhere.) There is not the barest suggestion of anything like this in the adventure novel; which cannot be an artistic fault. A tragic catharsis or one that overcomes the tragic must be present as a possibility from the very first moment and materialize before our eyes, while satiric and comic collisions, ironic-cathartic processes may take us by surprise. However, given our present restricted knowledge of the material, we would insist on the abstract and incomplete nature of any such correspondences. We do not wish to construct artificial parallels before the total character of *Krull* as a satyr-piece to the *Joseph* novels lies fully unfolded before us.

Yet given these reservations there is one marvellous scene of parody in the present text which we can recognize as belonging to this variety. We are thinking of the love-scene between Krull as a lift-boy and the wife of the Strasbourg merchant, Madame Houpflé, who as authoress of novels 'full of psychological insight, *pleins d'esprit, et des volumes de vers passionnés*' goes under the name of Diane Philibert. This scene, written after the *Joseph* novels, is a delicious parody on the tragic love-conflict between Mut-em-enet, the mistress of Peteprê's house, and Joseph. In both cases a woman of refined intellect and high social standing is irresistibly attracted by a 'servant'; in both cases the impotence of the husband forms the biological background to the desire. Mut-em-enet's true passion breaks into terrible tragedy, the *hubris* of Joseph's self-confidence and self-delight unleashing an entire personal and social underworld. She, a person of refinement is dragged through a hell of lies, slander, degradation and devilish sorcery. All these *motifs*, stripped of their tragic dignity, meet in the graceful satyr-play of the confidence man. Degradation becomes masochistic lust, the infernal spells turn into a play on the name of Hermes, the god of thieves (with whom, by the way, young Pharaoh also compares Joseph). Krull hears the name for the first time and solemnly adds it to his store of knowledge. When he confesses to his newly-acquired mistress his theft of her jewel-box at the customs, she asks him to steal it once again in her presence. Only then is the authoress Diane Philibert satisfied, certain that he will remain in her life for ever: 'Yes, when the grave covers us, me and you too, Armand, *tu vivras dans mes vers et dans mes beaux romans,* everyone of which— never breathe this to the world!—has been kissed by your lips. *Adieu, adieu, Chéri . . .*'

These individual instances are important because of the deeper connection between tragedy and satyr-play. Thomas Mann resurrects a mythical past in order to dramatize an education in pleasure: from the dangers of self-regarding to genuine self-delight in working for a human community. As we have shown, the *what* and *how* of this problem are determined by the historical perspective of the author. This perspective as such forms the premise of his optimism; without it there could be no development to maturity, stability and the enjoyment thereof. But, as we have again indicated, it is an abstract perspective, Utopian in its objective content. It reveals no concrete transitions to anything new in our reality; it hovers over the divisions and apparent impasse of our time, unable to fix itself anywhere. Yet by looking to a future it can shed a light on these and make manifest even in contemporary man the possibility of development, if simply as possibility.

Heinrich Mann's *Henri Quatre* is only apparently more realistic than *Joseph and his Brethren*. It presents a concrete historical past as a concrete model for today. But since the author's socialist perspective has not translated itself artistically, the effect is equally Utopian. The function of the myth in the *Joseph* novels is to give as concrete a picture as possible of the consequences for the present of Thomas Mann's perspective of the future. For this reason the cycle takes place both in an actual time, Mann's self-made mythical world, and outside time, that is outside history proper. Thomas Mann is not a party to modern myth-making; he arouses and quenches his myth simultaneously at every instant. It can, therefore, act as a realistic milieu for demonstrating the human consequences of his abstract perspective. For only the latter is Utopian; the milieu in which it is realized is a full-bodied artistic creation. Indeed, the main thing about Mann's work is its thorough lack of Utopianism. Only in the final analysis, after all the gliding journeys between myth and reality does *Joseph* emerge as a realistic illustration of an abstract perspective. The intent of this complex interaction between theme and form is to elicit and foster human possibilities, to give them an imaginary field in which to develop. They are real human possibilities, but incapable of proper growth in present-day capitalist and imperialist society, where their only form of expression is a lonesome longing. Whereas, elsewhere in Mann, from Thomas Buddenbrook to Adrian Leverkühn, irony and self-irony serve to unmask the grotesqueness of contemporary tragedies, here they create a mental world in which human abilities, otherwise doomed to misuse and frustration, can grow to their fullest capacity.

This must be understood before one can appreciate *Krull* as a satyr-piece. Its material is contemporary bourgeois society, of which it presents a very detailed portrait. How is the personality supposed to recover its self-enjoyment here? Does not this contradict all the experience a contemporary bourgeois encounters by day and by hour? No; for Mann's ironic and self-ironic criticism of bourgeois society has set itself an entirely new and original theme: in the world of the dying bourgeoisie only the confidence man can fulfil himself in pleasure. The idea itself marks a new level in Mann's criticism of society and the bourgeois class. When one thinks of the time at which *Krull* was first broached, one realizes how many ingrained illusions Mann had to shed, how fearfully he must have struggled with himself before the criticism implicit in *Krull* could mature and be made explicit; how much he broadened and deepened his gifts and outlook in the fight against fascism.

The type of confidence man as the only person who can enjoy himself today is the very opposite of those characters in the early Mann who were meant to embody an easy and irresponsible life. As we have seen they simply went to pieces both publicly and privately (e.g., Christian Buddenbrook and the hero of *The Bajazzo*). The difference between them and Krull is that they, for all their recklessness and irresponsibility, never overstepped the bounds of middle-class propriety, while he was quite shamelessly committing petty theft as a child, and if later on he was to have second thoughts about certain plans, then the reasons had nothing to do with bourgeois morality.

But Krull the confidence trickster belongs in a special class. When he recalls his continual stealing of sweets as a boy he repudiates any suggestion that this was common theft: '... though I have had to accept being labelled, especially by the law, with the same name as ten thousand others ...' He admits that it was the quality of what he stole that so irresistibly attracted him: 'but it was not alone their quality that enchanted me; even more it was the carrying over of my dream treasure into my waking life that made up the sum of my delight.' Similar *motifs* occur after the jewellery theft on the journey to Paris. Stanko, a fellow hotel employee, catches Krull examining his loot; he demands and receives a share of the proceeds. A temporary comradeship binds them but is dissolved with Krull's indifferent rejection of a plan to raid a villa in Neuilly.

One might treat these episodes as *post hoc* embellishments of rather more obvious causes (cowardice, etc.). But Krull's later life shows that there is considerably more to them; we are dealing with an important trait of character. Krull rises rapidly in the hotel hierarchy. He becomes a waiter and enchants all his customers, in particular the women, but not them alone. He is put twice to the test here, so that we can see what his real motives are; the first time with Eleanor Twentyman, the seventeen or eighteen-year-old daughter of a rich Birmingham business man, who falls passionately in love with him, wants to elope with him and have a child so that she can face her doting father with a *fait accompli* and receive his blessing. Krull uses all the tact and sympathy he can in this delicate situation to turn down the proposal: 'These are all preposterous dreams, and I do not intend on their account to abandon my course in life or take this by-path.'

Still more significant is the choice with which he is faced by Lord Strathbogie, a rich Scottish aristocrat. This ageing, lonely man also feels drawn to the pliant, attractive, obliging youth. Krull to his great astonishment learns that Strathbogie's loneliness and dissatisfaction with life have led him into self-denial, although, as his lordship says: 'Self-repudiation helps one to appreciate someone else.' Krull is appreciated; Strathbogie offers him the post of valet at a much higher salary than he receives in the hotel. As Krull hesitates, he plays his last card: 'I am childless and master of my own affairs. There have been cases of adoption—you might wake up one day as Lord Strathbogie and heir to my possessions.' But Krull has long made up his mind to decline the offer, and even with these glittering prospects he does not falter and settle for a 'by-path'. His private reason for refusing typifies the nature of Krull's career: 'The main thing was that a confident instinct within me rebelled against a form of reality that was simply handed down to me and was in addition sloppy—rebelled in favour of free play and dreams, self-

created and self-sufficient, dependent, that is, only on imagina·
tion.'

It is even clearer here than in the cases of Stanko or Eleanor
Twentyman that Krull's purpose is not to deceive in order to
enrich himself or climb the social ladder. As we have seen, moral
scruples mean little to him. Rather he becomes a confidence
trickster in order to live a life appropriate to his imagination, to
impose on life his image of himself. He wants victory and the
enjoyment thereof; money and social rank are no more than
(admittedly rather devious) ways of securing the necessary circumstances for the unhindered play of his talents. To create these
conditions Krull requires the confidence trick.

Part One ends with Krull's first big confidence trick. But here
again it is not on his initiative. This time it is the Marquis de
Venosta, whom Krull also serves as a waiter, who presents him
with a choice. True, Krull's own behaviour and manner of life
play an important part, yet not to the extent of winning over
Venosta and girl-friend in the restaurant.

At this period Krull is leading an innocent double life in Paris.
He acquires an elegant wardrobe and spends his free evenings
imitating the life of a gentleman in fashionable drinking-houses.
The two young men, roughly the same age, meet at a difficult
time for Venosta. His parents disapprove of his long-standing
relationship with a pretty Parisian actress and, to make the
separation as painless as possible, wish to send him, well-
endowed with money and recommendations, on a world tour.
Venosta cannot and will not break with the girl. As Krull, seem-
ing no more than a sympathetic listener, hears him out, the great
plan takes shape: Krull will take Venosta's place on the world
tour, write letters to his parents, etc.; Venosta in the meantime
can go on living incognito with his mistress in Paris. Now it is
characteristic of the Krull confidence trick that while he accepts
Venosta's allowance for the journey (20,000 francs), learns his
signature, etc., as a matter of course, he also as a matter of course
assures Venosta's existence in Paris with the 12,000 francs that

he has 'saved' from the Houpflé-Philibert affair. It does not surprise, therefore, that Venosta, a carefree aristocrat who has not considered the possibility of need, should be very moved and call him a gentleman. And indeed, it is obvious that the prospect of adventures to please and to test him means much more to Krull than the (not so substantial) material gain.

Krull presents the same physiognomy in the first stage of his trickster-life on his journey to Lisbon and in Lisbon itself; Part One ends with this sojourn. The centrepiece is his courtship of Zouzou, the interesting and pretty daughter of Kuckuck, the archaeology professor, which he pursues with a didactic-rhetorical gallantry (his courtship of her majestic Portuguese mother takes a rather earthier course). Krull stays many weeks longer in Lisbon than his programme permits simply in order to tame this mental and moral shrew and to teach her what real love is. (The fact that quite by-the-bye he obtains an audience with the king and 'earns' a Portuguese decoration with his charm only underlines the playful-purposeless character of his sojourn). He enters the courtship knowing full well that in his role as Marquis de Venosta he can neither marry nor enjoy an illicit relationship with Zouzou (not to mention the possibility of material gain). It is an adventure for the sake of adventure, a mental tournament in which to test his own powers and try them to the uttermost. If he can come through this battle of wits, if he can triumph over the difficulties and complications which he has set in his own path, then he will have won the right to enjoy his powers and his person.

This calls for great resourcefulness, an unfailing ability to mobilize just those talents which are required in any given, and never precisely calculable, situation. It calls for perspicacity, shrewdness, sensitivity to each and every case, the right note and measure and much more again. In a word, Krull must exert all his powers to appear convincing where Venosta does it simply by birth and upbringing. As a result he becomes much more interesting and 'genuine' than Venosta himself, simply because, while everyone takes him for the real Venosta, he must prove himself such at every instant. We take just one small example. Krull is invited by Zouzou to make up a tennis party, but he has never played tennis in his life; he has only once or twice set foot on a tennis court as a ball-boy. He therefore has to improvize a display of acrobatics in order to show the company that he is a true aristocrat who had once mastered the game but has not played for years. The real Venosta would either be able to play tennis or coldly declare that he could not. It is the same with the letter to his parents. It is a self-parodying miniature work of art. The real Venosta would have dashed off some simple and far less interesting report. Everywhere Krull is more 'genuine' than his original.

His ungenuineness, his trickery drive Krull to do things which would never enter the head of his model. His entire career from son of the house to liftboy, from waiter to man-of-the world forms an inextricable tangle of life and play-acting, of life as play and play as life, a *commedia dell'arte* transposed into life. This theatricality lends the whole an atmosphere of (relative) innocence which however never lets the crookery out of view. And innocence is not just a word here, an aesthetic cover-up or gloss. If Krull had really taken up the career of waiter and not just treated it as a temporary condition, a part to be played, a springboard to adventure; if, as a real Marquis, he had seriously pursued a court career or something similar and regarded his decoration not as an amusing ornament, a flourish to his role, he would have had to commit rather fouler things than hitherto. His mental and moral physiognomy would have suffered much more disfigurement in the hard struggle up the hotel or court ladder; while here, his very crookery and the provisional and unreal character of his existence enable him to avoid the relentless and humiliating demands of capitalist life and to change them into a graceful charade committing him to nothing.

This is a kind of art. But it never settles into a fixed perform-ance. Krull, who looks condescendingly on dillettantes, has a

131

deep respect for real achievement. He admires, for instance, Andromache, 'la fille de l'aire' in the Paris circus, but he also asks himself: is this height of perfection still human? Krull says no: 'She was not a woman; but she was not a man either and therefore not a human being. A solemn angel of daring with parted lips and dilated nostrils, that is what she was, an unapproachable Amazon of the realms of space beneath the canvas, high above the crowd, whose lust for her was transformed into awe.' Here we touch on the Tonio Kröger-Leverkühn sphere, but merely touch and, as in the Joseph novels, abandon it for life (a different life from the simple contrast with art that we meet from Klöterjahn through to Hans Hansen and Ingeborg Holm). In this respect, too, despite the ironic and self-ironic correspondence between Leverkühn and Andromache, *Krull, Confidence Man* is the satyr-play of the Joseph legend.

Thomas Mann, therefore, contrary to his *avant-garde* literary contemporaries, does not rule out the possibility that man even today may develop his latent capacities and thereby acquire the right to enjoy his personal existence. This optimism takes root in the perspective to which he has long and steadfastly adhered, but because of his penetrating realistic insight into the nature of bourgeois society it is scored with ironic reservation. He shows us the tragic and its conquest in the self-enjoyment of a realized personality, but to do so lifts out of history a fairy-tale reality of 'once-upon-a-time' and 'as-if-it-had-never-happened'. When he turns directly to the present we have the satyr-play of the confidence trickster who alone in bourgeois society is qualified to enjoy the fruits of his personality.

There is no parallel in the history of German literature, still less in the writing of our own day, for such buoyancy coupled with such accurate satire. One has to go back to the Dervish in Lessing's *Nathan* to find anything that would be even roughly analogous. But even here the difference stands out more than the similarity. Lessing's epilogue belongs to the dawn of the bourgeois ascendance in Germany before the French Revolution, a period therefore which imposed a few heroic illusions even on such a critic as he. The highest fulfilment of personality, its self-aware serenity dwells here with the beggar, the naked chess-playing pilgrim on the banks of the Ganges, who indeed poses an ironic critique of all the possible social virtues in the compass of the bourgeois horizon. But within the general attack against absolutism, feudalism and their ideologies such a critique can only play an episodic role. Should a similar attitude move into the centre, as later often happened with much lesser writers, then this kind of fulfilment must acquire a fatal tinge of resignation, indeed hypocrisy and social self-deception.

Mann's originality—his buoyancy, serenity and humour—springs from a true self-knowledge of the contemporary bourgeoisie. Thomas Mann speaks a truth about his relationship to bourgeois society and the value of that relationship for knowledge and creation when he writes, already in *Parisian Balance-Sheet*: 'I too, am a "burgher" ... But simply to know how it is historically with bourgeois life today means that one has already stepped beyond this form of life and cast a glance at something new. One underestimates self-knowledge, if one considers it idle, quietist or pietistic. No one remains quite what he was, when he knows himself.'

We hope we have shown how his socialist perspective, which consolidated itself much later, proved, however abstractly, a principle to spur and encourage him in the same direction. Naturally, we must add to this interpretation of *Krull* the important reservation that we do not know what the end of the story will be, so that we must not regard as final what we consider the essentials of character and story here. Krull's later inter-relationships with the world may so strengthen or weaken certain hitherto salient features as to modify all proportions and call into question or indeed falsify all conclusions drawn from the earlier part. Interpretation can only take nourishment from what is already created; beyond this it is empty guesswork.

Now that we have the first part of a great work of art, raising some of the most important questions of bourgeois existence in the present, we await its sequel with excitement. And such excitement is our best way of honouring and congratulating Thomas Mann on his eightieth birthday: in thinking of him on this day we look not to the past but to the future; we expect him to go on extending and deepening our picture of the world just as he has done in every previous work.

Spring 1955.

Postscript. Thomas Mann's untimely death alas nullifies our necessary reservations. One realizes with deep shock that the great satirical novel of our time remains uncompleted, that the story of Krull's youth must now pursue its life in world literature as a fragment. But there are torsos and torsos. The majority simply provide material for scholarly interpretation. In some we observe with a mixture of wonder and regret beginnings full of promise which suddenly break off at some, often accidental, point leaving us mentally and creatively guessing at what was to come. The figure of Krull awakens other feelings. The slender proportions, the serenity of youth are retained in the fragmentary and assured for posterity. This torso, like many remnants of classical sculpture, has its own irresistible charm, its own peculiar perfection simply as a torso, in its very incompleteness or fragmentariness of theme. Different and no doubt much less than what was planned, concluded before its time, this little that will be handed down to the ages is yet perfectly formed in itself.

Appendix A

ROYAL HIGHNESS

L IKE *Buddenbrooks*, this novel of Thomas Mann is also an epic of decline, but ... more of that later. Everything that Thomas Mann writes is instinct with decline, and this finds a perfect expression in the broad, tranquil, chronicle-like epic, stylized to a point of dryness. Thomas Mann's is a true epic tone, to be found elsewhere today only in Selma Lagerlöf and Henrik Pontoppidan, but Mann's epic and its bold horizons are much more consciously the result of perceptions in the present. I said Thomas Mann sees a decline; beneath the motionless surface he sees the invisible agents of destruction; he can so see and describe a day in a person's life that we are made to feel by the movement of small, ordinary, objectively drawn events their downhill course. And the big, powerful moments simply throw into relief and recognition something for which, inwardly, we are already prepared though we may not be aware of or indeed admit it. Thomas Mann sees the connection between all things; he makes the smallest details significant, though not (as in Zola, for instance) by torturing a little thing into a romantic symbol of an entire life, but by showing that the whole of life really does consist of nothing but such minutiae and that should one of these, as a result of a thousand similar little things of bygone years, accidentally release some long pent-up emotions, then this small event becomes a symbol for the whole; so that if one of them (and again accidentally) recurs rather more frequently and noticeably we should similarly feel it to be symbolic. This is the monumentality of a grey monotony, an endless monotony and triviality; suggesting, however, that the almost limitless multitude of small and grey events that make up the actual novel is no more than an infinitesimal part of the endless monotony of life itself, which gives this particular monotony its endlessness and monumentality. And the way these things are related underlines this still more: the very lack of emphasis, the chronicle-like manner, the dry seriousness, the impartiality of which they are spoken, the unaccented, unselective tone makes the smallest of them important.

Naturally, Thomas Mann is nevertheless not 'objective'. As in every genuine writer his objectivity is no more than a gesture concealing lyricism. But it is a peculiar love, a remarkable longing for life that speaks from this dry impartiality—he describes it himself in *Tonio Kröger*. It is a love of life, but 'life' here means simplicity, simple happiness, simple satisfaction, an ability to take one's place unquestioningly in the course of things, a simple sense of belonging to a human community. Thomas Mann gives us the poetry of things while he hides behind it, for he is a little ashamed of this love. And not only for reasons of natural shame, but also because love which yearns is without hope, because Mann knows what his dying Lorenzo de Medici only senses from Savonarola's words: 'I hear a song: my own song, the deep low song of longing. Girolamo, yet do you not know me? Whither the longing urges, there one is not, that one is not—you know? And yet man likes to confuse himself with his longing.' This perhaps Thomas Mann always knew, perhaps also that one may not love the simplicity of things as he does, seeking out the simplest simplicity and the most muted ordinariness with such longing, tenderness and understanding; that ordinary life is much more 'interesting' than his yearning eyes perceive, and would mistake this love and feel insulted. Therefore he must conceal it.

But objectivity can perhaps never exist without a certain irony. The most serious regard for things is always somewhat ironic, for somewhere or other the great gulf between cause and effect, between the conjuring of fate and the fate conjured must become obvious. And the more natural the peaceful flow of things appears, the truer and deeper this irony will be. Admittedly it is only in *Buddenbrooks* that this emerges so clearly and, as it were, from a single source. In the later writings this irony of Mann takes on differing forms, yet its deepest root remains this feeling of dislocation from, and longing for, the great natural vegetative community. The new and varying ironic tone stems from the tragi-comic unrealizability of the various kinds of longing as such, from the amusing tragedies of separateness and isolation that occur when such longing does come into contact with life. Life now (though its essence still remains 'the ordinary') is more complexly conceived, much more elusive of categories; causing diverse tragedies and meting out crueller and more laughable fates to those it does not recognize. In Mann's stories and dramatic essays (one can hardly call *Fiorenza* anything else) the poetry of things speaks to us in a lyrical tone; we hear a many-voiced longing for life, and the great oppositions sharpen to grotesque extremes, assume fantastic confrontations. But because these are many and life is all of them it is difficult to break off any one fragment from the whole and let it stand separately for life. This can only succeed in episodes, tragi-comic adventures, grotesque *dénouements*; it can only succeed completely in cases of caricature, even where the caricature is fundamentally symbolic. But the best and deepest instances will not finally separate off from the great community. Only once (in *Tristan*) does Mann manage to give the theoretical focus, which unites individual case and community, a deeply ironic form. In the best conceived cases theory remains theory and breaks up the form of the drama and the story. Only in the big epic does his structure need no theoretical repair, for here he is not compelled to compress the vastness of life into a forced symbol; the tragedy of slow decline along a gradual slope need not be summarized in a single situation. And yet it has taken him seven years since the appearance of his first great novel to give us his long-awaited second.

At first one is struck by the similarity. The same tone, the same attitudes and a similar pattern of experiences with similar characters. The decline of a family is also the theme of this novel. The family as the unit and focus of life provides the frame, and the small events in the life of a family, the christenings, worries over the children's education, the struggles of the parents and the deeds that mark out their lives, these are the stations which tell us how time passes and the family declines. Deaths and births are signs of the slow continuity of life. And at the same time they are signs of decline: of changing values, conduct and attitudes. This development goes from naïve assurance to conscious stylization, and here lies the seed of decay. For the conscious gesture may at any moment turn into the ironic, and what was done for the sake of irony may turn into self-parody—and from here it is only a step to loss of control and complete decadence. For life means being born into a community and fulfilling its duties. Once these are questioned, once their infallibility is called into doubt, once they have to be romanticized to be found beautiful so that one may live by them, then decadence has set in. And each question isolates the questioner, each romanticization separates him from his romanticized object. As soon as the bond snaps between man (or, better, the community of men, the family) and the cause for which he lives, whatever else unites them disintegrates. Man perishes as soon as he has nothing to live by.

But what took place there in a Lübeck patrician family, continually making us feel (even if it was never said) that the same tragedy had already occurred in a neighbouring house and would overtake another in the next generation—this we experience here in the story of a small German princely family. The difference of subject-matter in the two novels determines the difference of their form, and it is a testimony to Mann's art that it would be difficult to say what is cause and what effect. I could present the situation as follows: Mann appears more of a *Novelle* writer here than seven years ago; keener, more pointed, posing his situations and conflicts with greater abstraction. Hence the subject of this novel is the story of a family much more loosely connected with the outside world than in the other novel, and its typicality is only theoretical: we simply know that it is typical and that there are similar cases elsewhere. But with equal justice I could say: this is about a princely family, whose social position therefore raises it out of the ordinary community and so makes its life fantastic, irrational, 'interesting'. And the great distance from human community at which it is forced to live gives each contact and meeting a *Novelle*-like edge, making major events of them in precisely the terms of the theoretically typical. This novel then is more compact than the first. To take simply as an example: as against four generations it treats only two. Its episodes are more independent, although the main story is simpler and more straightforward. The characters are more sharply differentiated and the atmosphere less pervaded by them. The clearer emphases indeed disclose certain mannerisms—some features are overdrawn and there is a too frequent and too obvious use of symbolical atmospherics. But this is only here and there; one's foremost feeling is, together with the similar richness, one of greater compression.

In the first novel conduct and gesture were simply signs of one's relationship to things; here they form the content of life. The decline which there took place before our eyes, quietly turning characters into figure-heads of what they once were, here constitutes the premise, the point of departure. The princely calling: the fine gestures accompanying what can very well do without them, the ceremony not needed for ordinary matters. The gesture therefore separates itself entirely from action and so becomes a problem of life, unabstracted. Further, since it involves no question of utility, the problem of calling is posed with greater firmness and clarity. Here gesture is vocation and profession, function is the content of life. Prince Johann

Albrecht, somewhat naïvely, still accords his 'high duties' a measure of trust, but in his two sons we already see the outlines of two types of decline. Albrecht, the elder, the more typical and intelligent sees through the emptiness and aimlessness of his ceremonial manners; he looks down on the life of others, the life he neither knows nor can know. And with tranquil arrogance he passes on all his duties to his younger brother, Klaus Heinrich; he withdraws and will vanish from life as if he had never existed. Klaus Heinrich still accepts his 'high calling' as a duty, but how much of this is acquired, theoretical, the enjoyment (of which he is naïvely aware, but nevertheless aware) of its and his purely decorative effect!

Fulfilment of duty here isolates man perhaps even more than its neglect, thereby adding a deeper irony to Mann's central problem. Life as ceremony separates itself off from ordinary life, and it becomes impossible to restore their original unity. Albrecht abdicates for life—and this perhaps is why he looks with such deep contempt upon his ceremonial manners, condemned to perpetual sterility. Klaus Heinrich's most painful experience is his attempt as a young man to rid himself of the manners which separate him from others, to be as they are. Pain and ridicule are the result; those who dazzle with ceremony are also condemned to a life of ceremony; life cruelly thrusts them back into the brilliance that is their fate. Christian Buddenbrook perished because he no longer felt bound by the traditions into which he was born, and his brother because he wished and was able to do violence to his rebellious instincts. But in this world there is no question even of struggle; it is gone, dissolved into nothingness. And the man who wants to escape from the path his birth prescribes is not even a comic figure.

Klaus Heinrich nevertheless would like to find out about life, at least to catch a few glimpses, and the tragedy whereby the obligations of his 'high calling' increase and his desire and ability to excurse into life diminish is drawn with a fine irony. But then the miracle occurs, the great chance . . .

This novel is not only more like a *Novelle* than the first in technique, but also in theme. There everything was equally and typically grey; here the decisive event is coloured and irrational as in a *Novelle*. An ailing American dollar king settles in the small principality, Klaus Heinrich falls in love with his daughter, marries her and the old man's millions rescue the small state from bankruptcy. The way Thomas Mann assimilates this *Novelle* element to his theme, removing any effect of chance or surprise, making it merge with the ordinary course of events is quite amazing. The link is the community of experience. The old millionaire also belongs to a second and declining generation, no longer sure of what it should be doing and aiming at; he flees from this unbearable situation to Europe. His daughter lives in the same isolation as Klaus Heinrich, is animated by the same wish to look into life and get to know it; the same pressure drives her back into loneliness. And just as form for Klaus Heinrich means the chill decorative motions, the professed interest, the bored question asked out of kindness, a form of which his life will consist, so for her it is an ironic intellectual opposition to all things. And she feels the necessity of this form so strongly that while she continually ironizes the vulnerable and not-very-intelligent Klaus Heinrich, she on no account would wish him to defend himself; this is only *her* form, Klaus Heinrich has another; he does not need to be intelligent and quick-witted.

However, this sympathy and understanding would soon cool, remaining just an episode in their lives (for the girl does not believe that Klaus Heinrich really loves her—and no Klaus Heinrich could go on loving hopelessly forever), if life did not after all open up to them and offer plentiful instruction. The bond that unites them diminishes still further the *Novelle* character of the Americans' role, for it is their most fantastic and improbable feature, namely their enormous wealth. A minister of the small *Land* discloses the financial situation to Klaus Heinrich, suggesting how important his marriage would be, how much his people, his beloved, loyal people looked forward to it. Klaus Heinrich grows serious, and from his first serious feeling springs his 'high calling', a gesture. The girl feels that what is going on inside him touches her, too, and will not reject it as she has rejected every other experience in the past. Klaus Heinrich not only studies law himself, but gives the girl instruction, too, and the books on national economy bring to pass what Klaus Heinrich has so much longed for. Soon the happy little *Land* congratulates them on their engagement, and the father-in-law redeems a few hundred million marks worth of debt accumulated by the *Land*.

Yet there is something about this ending which leaves a slightly unpleasant feeling, and it is perhaps worthwhile examining it more closely. I think the reason is that it belongs to a different subject-matter from the rest of the novel. The characters are seen in too decadent a light for them to find happiness or the prospect of happiness quite so easily. The course of the novel, as we watched the various histories, led our gaze slowly downwards, and the end suddenly brought this movement to a halt. The novel itself creates this inescapable incline, which then suddenly ceases. The end blocks the progression which the novel has set in motion. Its tempo, too, differs from that of the rest. As we have already said, the essential tempo is that of slow, imperceptible advance, natural growth and decay. Suddenly a new turn is taken with the possibility of further changes, whereas we have been taught by the novel that only expected things happen, that there are no new changes and possibilities, only the slow unfolding of the old. Mann's epic technique will not sustain this sudden ending (even in this heightened and concentrated form). The natural ending here can only be the slow filtering of sand from the upper to the lower half of an hour-glass; perhaps an ending is quite unnecessary, for the flow of things—'tempo is direction', Kipling once quotes as the words of a German officer—itself shows us the end. In a word, Mann in his new novel has proved unable to overcome finally the *Novelle* character of his theme.

But the weakness of the end only weakens the
affect one's picture of the whole. Mann's monume
in the magnificence of his perceptions and not in
ence of his plots, his conceptions. That is, the percep
their grandeur latterly, growing and feeding on th
the plots. This unprogrammatic, unintentional cha
his first novel the deepest typicality, a universality tr
time. Yet this does not mean that the more 'interes
and the more 'interesting' characters and the occasiona
isms of the second novel turn it into an ordinary 'in
novel which loses value once the 'interest' grows a bi
bare. Mann's writing never feels quite new, it never s
reading him that the ink is not quite dry. There is in his
that now vanishing sense of bourgeois, patrician dignit
dignity which derives from the slow movement of solid v

A review (1909).

Appendix B

THOMAS MANN ON THE LITERARY HERITAGE

THE battle for heritage is one of the most important ideological tasks of anti-fascism in Germany. National Socialism has used its state power and monopoly of the legal press in order to falsify in the most ruthless manner Germany's entire political and cultural past. From university to primary school, from the fat 'learned' tome to the small, popular, crudely demagogic pamphlet this work of falsification has proceeded on a large and systematic scale. The demagogy of mass propaganda has no qualms about turning every great figure of the past into a simple forerunner of National Socialism. The most blatant ignorance, the most squalid mendacity characterize this kind of literature, as a textbook example of which we would quote Fabricius's book on Schiller. This literature banks on the unfamiliarity of the broad masses with the great figures of the past and their trusting acceptance of the official fascist propaganda.

No less dangerous, at least, is the more 'refined', 'scholarly' way of falsifying the past. To this end National Socialism has mobilized the entire resources of the universities and the straitjacketed 'free' literature. There were not a few voluntary *Führers* to take charge of this trend, having already fitted the past to a reactionary interpretation, which matched the political aims of fascism, before Hitler came to power. It suffices if one thinks of writers like Spengler, Klages, Baeumler in whose wake a considerable amount of this refined and concealed falsification was done. These writers do not suddenly break with the literary

144

and literary-historical traditions of the last few decades. On the contrary, they follow on quite consciously from the well-known theoreticians of the imperialist period, Dilthey, Gundolf, etc. The falsification of the German past pretends to be saving the honour of this past from its former 'rationalist', 'liberal' derogation. And the reactionary tendency only appears directly as slander or omission in certain cases; in cases of such obviously revolutionary figures as cannot be given a reactionary 'interpretation' (Heine). But where period, trend, language, individual peculiarities afford the slightest chance of 'interpreting' revolutionary figures into their opposite, fascist literary history makes every effort to appropriate and include them among the precursors of fascism (Thomas Münzer, Hölderlin, Georg Büchner). In these circumstances Thomas Mann's book of essays on Goethe, Richard Wagner, Cervantes, Platen and Storm (*Sufferings and Greatness of the Masters*, Berlin 1934[1]) is of extreme importance. All the more because the book appeared in Germany itself and not in emigration, so that there were no police obstacles to prevent its spread and influence. The subject-matter too is of extreme topicality. Goethe and Wagner after all play a central part in the National-Socialist myth of German literature. Therefore, a non-fascist, anti-fascist analysis which reveals the true character and significance of such figures in the history of German culture has an importance transcending the purely literary.

There is no doubt that Mann's essays are anti-fascist. (Admittedly, with the exception of the Cervantes essay, which belongs to 1934, they were written before Hitler came to power, in 1932 and 1933.) The essential aim of all these essays is anti-fascist: Mann's main concern is once more the defence of humanism against barbarism. In Thomas Mann's eyes the great figures of the past owe their greatness not so much to their formal skill

---

[1] Not published under this title in English; the essays are to be found, some separately, some together in *Past Masters* and *Essays of Three Decades*.

but to their forthright and generous defence and furtherance of humanist tendencies, their struggle against all threats of barbarism. Thomas Mann concedes nothing to the ruling fascist trend which disguises the Third Reich as a non-bourgeois era and finds the past full of similar attempts to shake off 'bourgeois civilization' (in the fascist sense). In particular, he traces Goethe's humanism to his bourgeois being, his bourgeois way of life and outlook. And with the writers of the nineteenth century, whom he treats, he similarly combats the reactionary-fascist defamation of the important artistic tendencies and achievements of the bourgeoisie in the nineteenth century.

This campaign against barbarism on behalf of humanism is certainly a central ideological problem of the anti-fascist struggle, and it does great credit to Thomas Mann for having taken it up at this point. Nevertheless, the effectiveness and potency of his struggle to rescue humanism is weakened by a serious lack of clarity in his central position. Thomas Mann does not see the inseparable connection between bourgeois humanism and bourgeois revolution.

Bourgeois humanism arose in the heroic period of the emancipation of the bourgeois class, and when the fire of this revolutionary enthusiasm flickered out, bourgeois humanism too inevitably lost its light and warmth. The great importance of Heine's prose writings, his treatment of philosophy and religion in Germany lies in the fact that he recognized the connection between humanism and revolution with great clarity and gave it central place.

It would, of course, be an exaggeration and do Thomas Mann an injustice to suggest that he saw nothing of this connection. But he makes the disastrous mistake, itself so much a part of the development of German ideology, of denying the relevance of this connection for Germany and German literature. In Schiller's revolutionary humanism Mann sees something French, while he regards Goethe's humanism as typically German. Starting from here Mann draws a parallel between Goethe and Schiller which is so important for his basic conception that we must quote it in detail : 'It is characteristic of the French literary mind, described (by Schiller, G.L.) in few words, this peculiar inter- weaving of the humanitarian and revolutionary strain, of gener- ous faith in mankind, together with the deepest, bitterest, yes, most mocking pessimism, concerning individual man. He defines abstract, political-humanitarian passion, contrasting it with the sense-born realism of individual sympathy. He is the patriot of humanity, with the humanitarian, revolutionary spirit.' One can therefore, according to Thomas Mann, call Goethe 'funda- mentally German and fundamentally unpatriotic, while Schiller is an international patriot. He represents the bourgeois ideal in the political and democratic sense; Goethe, on the other hand, in the intellectual and cultural one.'

Despite the very perceptive individual remarks here, the parallel nevertheless reveals a dangerous tendency which, of ob- jective necessity, often contrary to Mann's intentions, leads to a false estimate of cultural development in Germany. For given these premises Thomas Mann must end up by intellectually glorifying Goethe's conservatism and indeed smacking of con- servatism himself. 'Goethe', he goes on to argue, 'defended society in the conservative sense, which is inherent in the con- ception of defence. One cannot be unpolitical, one can only be anti-political, and that means conservative, while the spirit of politics is in itself humanitarian and revolutionary.' In all this Mann on the one hand underestimates the progressive elements in Goethe's outlook as a whole, although in other places he himself stresses them with praiseworthy inconsistency. On the other, he is compelled to see in later German conservatism and nationalism an 'excrescence' of this justified 'fundamentally German', essentially Goethean tendency. He robs himself there- fore of the ability to offer a thorough and correct critique of the reactionary trends of the second half of the nineteenth century which he recognizes with relative clarity.

This erroneous conception of German development in the

nineteenth century naturally has its deep social roots. The great epoch of German literature and philosophy is a period preparatory to bourgeois revolution where the objective conditions of revolution were not yet present. Thus the tempestuous, impatient, sometimes dogmatically blind subjectivism of some of the great figures of this period does not require to be imported from France, but is a necessary product of these German conditions. And to complement this, the conservative aims of other great men of this period (first and foremost, Goethe and Hegel) are always attempts to implement the social and cultural content of the bourgeois revolution, the humanism of this period in a non-revolutionary way. By simply labelling Goethe a conservative, Mann makes an inconsistent and impermissible concession to the ruling ideologies of his time.

These ideologies grow out of the defeat of the 1848 revolution, when the German bourgeoisie betrayed its own revolution, and out of the reactionary solution of the central question of the bourgeois revolution in Germany—the achievement of national unity by Bismarck's Prussia. The German bourgeoisie which affirmed the political development of Germany after 1870 required an ideology which would increasingly dissociate itself from the revolutionary humanism of the 1848 period. A deep break occurs in Germany's cultural development; the most resolute adherents of revolutionary humanism draw the most varied conclusions. I shall mention only one example, Heinrich Mann, Thomas Mann's brother, whose political and cultural radicalism led him to seek a contemporary German heritage in the literary development of France, to link himself with the social, political and cultural traditions that ran from Voltaire to Zola and Anatole France.

In his criticism of the ruling German ideology Thomas Mann never goes as far as his brother. Therefore his attitude towards the main questions of historical development, determining choice and evaluation of a heritage, is more uncertain and contradictory than Heinrich Mann's. This contradiction is immediately apparent in his view of the bourgeois as the essential characteristic of the great writers of the nineteenth century. His justified and correct attitude suffers from an unusually contradictory conception of the bourgeois. A significant feature of Mann's humanism is his sense that bourgeois society cannot be the final form of human development. He is also right in discovering features in late Goethe, which coincide with certain aims of the great Utopians, and in connecting Goethe's ambition for a world literature with these social aims. In emphasizing the importance of these views of Thomas Mann, we lay stress on the desire to transcend the bourgeois horizon and not on whether we can agree with his entire argument and method. In this sense let us quote an important passage from his book: 'The bourgeois attitude passes over into that of a world community by virtue of technical and rational utopianism; it passes over—if one takes the word broadly enough and is willing to understand it undogmatically—into the communistic . . . The burgher is lost, and loses touch with the new or coming world, if he cannot bring himself to part from the life-destroying, easy-going ideologies that still condition him, and address himself stoutly to the future. The new, the social world, the organized, planned and unified world in which humanity will be freed from such human, unnecessary burdens, injurious to self-respect and common sense; this world will come. . . . It will come, for an outward and rational order of things, adequate to the stage which human intelligence has now reached, must be created, or—in the worst case—be established by violent revolution, in order that the things of the soul may once more be justified.'

Such views represent the best heritage of German humanism. Unfortunately, Mann is not everywhere true to them. His estimate of post-1848 development and its significant representatives leads him to a quite different concept of the bourgeois and into making very serious concessions to the reactionary ideology of the imperialist period.

Mann clearly sees many dubious sides to the figure of Richard

Wagner. But nowhere will he stringently criticize the attitudes of his heroes after 1848. He not only everywhere seeks excuses, but also reasons for transfiguring Wagner's capitulation to the triumphant Hohenzollern regime (in 1848 Wagner was a revolutionary and fought on the Dresden barricades): 'Wagner was a good enough politician to link his affairs with the Bismarck empire; he saw in it an incomparably successful feat, and he attached his own fortunes to its chariot. The European hegemony of his art has become the cultural equivalent to the political hegemony of Bismarck.'

On the face of it this sounds simply a statement of fact. But Thomas Mann unfortunately finds a theory to fit. He says of Wagner: 'He went the way of the German bourgeoisie: from the revolution to disillusionment, to pessimism and a resigned power-protected inwardness.' This 'power-protected inwardness' is the attempt to harmonize the cultural heritage of the ascendant period of the German bourgeoisie with the Bismarck regime, with capitulation to this regime and its successors. The term 'power' on the one hand tacitly acknowledges that the Bismarckian form of the German Reich no longer corresponds, either politically or socially, to the old ideals of the German middle class; on the other it does rather more than terminological obeisance to the ideology which unreservedly acclaims the new period (the idea of the 'power-state' in Treitschke and the Ranke school, etc). Again, the restriction of the cultural heritage to 'inwardness' characterizes the tendency to retain from German classicism only that which can be brought into harmony with the isolated individual, who has withdrawn from politics and social activity, into harmony therefore with the capitulation of the bourgeoisie to the Bismarck regime, with the betrayal by the bourgeoisie of its own bourgeois revolution. His affirmation of this 'power-protected inwardness' forms the weak side to Mann's whole cultural conception and stands in crying contradiction to the broad perspective of future development which he gives in his earlier analysis. This last attitude indeed provides an ideological handle to any and every compromise with whatever force is in power, to every kind of capitulation, to a contemporary revival of 'the German abjectness'.[1]

Obviously, Thomas Mann is quite right to avoid dismissing Wagner's development after 1848 with a few cavilling, scornful words, in the manner of many Nietzschean fanatics. But he goes the wrong way about it, methodologically, in trying to explain the ideological weaknesses of the late Wagner, his capitulation to Christian religion and Hohenzollern nationalism, by the presence of religious and nationalist elements in pre-1848 Wagner. There is clearly a fundamental difference between a politically-radical adherent of Feuerbach before 1848, with strong, as yet unsurmounted, religious tendencies, and someone who both capitulates to the Bismarck regime and glorifies the Catholic religion in his work. There is equally a fundamental difference between a revolutionary who, however confusedly, derives his patriotism from the central problem of the bourgeois revolution in Germany—national unity, and the Wagner who after 1870 places this patriotism at the service of the Hohenzollern monarchy. If aided by theory and generalization, as it unfortunately is here, this manner of defence of a significant, but tragically broken, historical figure must turn into a misjudgment of history itself. In analysing the later Wagner Mann starts out from the attested historical fact that the origins of theatre and drama are religious. But in his eagerness to defend Wagner he reverses the order of development: 'I do believe that the secret longing and ultimate ambition of all theatre is to return to the bosom of the ritual out of which—in both the pagan and the Christian world—it sprang. The art of the theatre is already baroque, it is Catholicism, it is the Church; and an artist like Wagner, used to dealing with symbols and elevating monstrances, must have ended by feeling like a brother of priests, like a priest himself.'

[1] *deutsche Misere*: a phrase, coined by Heine and used frequently by Marx.

This development of drama certainly fits Wagner himself and the general trend in Germany after 1848 (Hebbel, Hauptmann, Hofmannsthal, Paul Ernst). But Thomas Mann's task should have been to discover and elaborate the reasons which determined this development. His uncritical generalization of this modern German trend leads him to historically wrong conclusions, for the two greatest epochs of the theatre—the Greek and the Shakespearean—took precisely the opposite direction. From religious, ritualistic beginnings they proceed directly into the irreligious, indeed to open struggle with a religious outlook. And in the great periods this turn to the anti-religious did not simply conclude a development; the beginning of real drama is full of such tendencies—think of Aeschylus's *Prometheus* or Marlowe.

Such objections to Mann's critical method and historical judgment in no way invalidate his desire to do justice to, and not simply dismiss, a figure of Wagner's significance. With this aim, we repeat, we are in full agreement; we consider it fruitful for the question of heritage. But for it to be really fruitful, we need clarity about the objectively tragic situation in which the important writers of Germany, who experienced the 1848 revolution with a sense of aspiration, found themselves after its defeat, after its betrayal by the German bourgeoisie. The history of German literature in this period provides a whole number of moving tragedies, tragedies of great writers who came to grief as a consequence of this development, who because of this break never reached the height their talent promised them. Apart from Wagner I shall mention Hebbel, Otto Ludwig; the later Heine, the career of Gottfried Keller also suffered certain modifications. To see the greatness of these figures in their right light one would need a literary approach the equal in sensitivity and understanding of Thomas Mann's defence of Wagner in decline; which would explain these tragedies in terms of the objective circumstances and subjective peculiarities of the individual writer. Although Mann clearly recognizes certain signs

of decadence in Wagner, the concept of 'power-protected inwardness', the notion that ideological compromise with the
Hohenzollern monarchy could possibly produce a great literature
(or philosophy) prevents him from saying anything really
decisive.

The consequences that flow from this attitude are particularly
important when it comes to judging the problem of realism in
literature. Once again, Mann's intention is right in always comparing Wagner with the important realists of the second half of
the nineteenth century, in particular Zola and Ibsen. This saves
him, happily, from that vulgarizing sociological simplification
of the problem of realism which so damaged the criticism of
German literature especially (refusing to consider any writer a
realist who showed pronounced unrealist or anti-realist tendencies, e.g., the 'down with Schiller' slogan in both German
naturalism and a phase of Russian theoretical development).

Thomas Mann is right to stress the impossibility of properly
judging the late Wagner without considering these realistic
elements in his creative method. But the way he applies himself
to this is inconsistent on two counts. First, he does not examine
the particular conditions of Zola's and Ibsen's development and
so neglects the more-marked realist tendencies in them as compared with Wagner. And this more-marked realism is obviously
not simply a quantitative more, but involves qualitatively
different creative methods. Secondly, Mann takes the weaknesses, the mystical and symbolic propensities in the creative method
of Zola and Ibsen as his basis of comparison. Initially, since he
is out to defend Wagner and not treat him as a tragic victim of
German conditions, these weak and inconsistent sides to, say,
Zola's realism provide him with effective arguments; but then
rebound on his central theoretical case, making it more confused
and driving him to false conclusions.

This is how he compares Zola and Wagner: 'It is not only
the love of size, the propensity to the grandiose and lavish; not
only, in the sphere of technique, the Homeric leit-motif that

they have in common. More than anything else it is a naturalism that amounts to the symbolic and the mythical. Who can fail to see in Zola's epic the tendency to symbol and myth that gives his characters their over-lifesize air? That Second Empire Astarte, Nana, is she not symbol and myth? Where does she get her name? It sounds like the babbling of primitive man. Nana was a cognomen of the Babylonian Ishtar: did Zola know that? So much the more remarkable and significant, if he did not.'

This conception is not only very important for the methodology of literary history and the evaluation of Wagner and his contemporaries; it also forms the basis for Mann's approach to the whole problem of contemporary realism. In regarding myth, the making and imagining of contemporary myths, as a legitimate and topical principle of contemporary realism, he follows this conception to its logical end. He combats the view of myth and psychology as constituting mutually contradictory principles in realist literature, and thereby (though not explicitly, and probably without being conscious of it) reduces the principles of realism to psychology. So, in his theory, he uncritically contributes to that impoverishment of modern realism which dominates the second half of the nineteenth century.

This tendency to combine myth and psychology leads him, via his defence of the Wagnerian synthesis, to make far-reaching concessions to the pseudo-realistic currents dominant today. He says of the combination of psychology and myth: 'The present day takes pleasure in asserting their essential incompatibility ... Indeed, psychology does seem too much a matter of reason to admit of our seeing in it anything but an obstacle in the path into the land of myth. And it passes as the antithesis of the mythical as of the musical—yet precisely this complex, of psychology, myth and music, is what confronts us, an organic reality, in two great cases, Nietzsche and Wagner.'

That this view is more than an accidental statement may be read just as clearly in Mann's remarks on his new mythical novel-cycle *Joseph and his Brethren*, as in his critical writing. In his judgment, too, of important contemporaries, he shows the same weakness that we established in the case of Wagner. In his article greeting Gerhart Hauptmann's seventieth birthday Mann recognizes clearly enough how much Hauptmann has moved from the socially-critical attitudes of his youth. But this Mann does not simply record, he extols it. He speaks of 'the deeply, authentically German stuff' of Hauptmann's imagination 'which despite the declared Republicanism and notwithstanding the naturalistic Socialism of *The Weavers* and *The Rats* was more at home in the infinite, the cosmic than in the world of society'. Social criticism, therefore, as practised by writers of Hauptmann's rank in the Latin countries, must 'retreat before this gentle, humid gaze upon the metaphysical and mystical'. 'But,' asks Thomas Mann, 'metaphysical Germanness and social commitment—are these incompatible? And especially in the case of Hauptmann?' (*Neue Rundschau* 1932, November).

Well, now it has become quite clear where this 'gentle, metaphysical retreat' leads. However, it is not Mann's mistake in Hauptmann's case that is important so much as his (unfortunately consistent) application of that historical attitude, which saw in Schiller's political freedom-pathos a 'French', not a truly German tendency, and which accepted German development after 1848, the mythification of social and historical problems, without real criticism.

This puts Thomas Mann, as a defender of the great traditions of humanism and literary realism against fascist barbarism, against the demagogic pseudo-realism and anti-realism of the National Socialists, in a difficult and at times extraordinarily weak position. For myth, particularly in its Wagnerian and Nietzschean version, forms a central plank in the German fascist 'theory' of myth. However much Thomas Mann may hate and despise the falsity and mendacity, the decadent barbarism of German fascism, he cannot effectively combat the central positions of fascist cultural barbarism from these theoretical starting-points. In all the essential political, cultural and literary questions he stands firmly opposed to fascism; but his historical outlook and its consequences on his attitude to a realist creative method weakens his polemic in the extreme.

This came out clearly in the discussions on Thomas Mann's *Joseph* novel, which was described as mythical. The fascist critics instinctively sensed the contradictions in the theme and tried to discredit Mann's new work as much as they could. Mann's defenders were put into a theoretically false position, for they were compelled to oppose Mann's 'myth' to the fascist myths, instead of unmasking the falsity of the entire myth conception of fascism. One of these critics, for instance, E. H. Gast, points out that the fascist criticism shows 'how disturbing it is for the makers of the new "myth of the twentieth century" to encounter the old myth'. And he concludes his comparison between Mann's myth and that of the fascists by saying 'that they have exactly the same relationship to one another as mentality or "attitude" to inspiration, as what is made to what is created' (*Die Sammlung*, Amsterdam, January 1934). Gast, therefore, in a very eclectic way, opposes Mann's 'good' myth to Rosenberg's 'bad' one.

Thomas Mann himself is not entirely blameless for this theoretically weak position of his defenders. The line of development of German literature drawn in this book goes from Goethe through Schopenhauer to Wagner and Nietzsche. Mann thereby makes Nietzsche (despite individual criticisms) the central theoretical figure in modern development. As far as this remains a statement of fact about bourgeois literature and philosophy in Germany, Thomas Mann is right: Nietzsche is indeed the most influential thinker and writer of the last several decades in Germany. The point is, however, which direction does this influence take, who are his consistent and legitimate successors? This is not a question of Nietzsche's intellectual level or stylistic talents. I myself have tried to show that Nietzsche is not to be wished away by a sleight of the hand or a few phrases

(*Nietzsche as Forerunner of Fascist Aesthetics* in *Contributions to a History of Aesthetics*).[1] But I also showed that the nub of Nietzsche's philosophy is the philosophical argument for barbarism which fascism turned into a terrible political and cultural reality. Nietzsche uses the classical heritage in order to barbarize it at a high intellectual level, to destroy all the bridges between the revolutionary humanism of the classical period of human development and imperialist ideology. Thus, by looking to Nietzsche for theoretical support in his humanist endeavours, in his struggle against fascist barbarism, Mann seeks a source which cannot help him. In intellect, culture, talent, insight and honesty Thomas Mann towers above any fascist ideologist—yet fascist consequences will always follow more consistently from Nietzsche than anti-fascist ones.

It is a significant and interesting personal trait of Thomas Mann that his development has proceeded without leaps, as an organic growth. To this peculiarity we owe his important realist achievements. Yet it has already once landed him in a dangerous situation: in the World War this slow organic growth could not keep pace with the tempestuous development of history, and Mann only belatedly linked himself with the democratic currents of his age. We believe that Thomas Mann's development is similarly threatened today. He is slow to overcome those elements of feeling and outlook which go back with him over a long period, his growth at times is too organic and plant-like. Philosophically and critically he is slower to come to terms with the new world situation than he is either politically or creatively. There are indeed signs of such a change, such a recasting in the present book. Earlier we quoted the interesting passage about the growth of bourgeois humanism beyond the bourgeois. And in the Cervantes essay, written after Hitler's advent to power, there is already some indication that Thomas Mann has begun to take a more critical attitude to Nietzsche in particular. At

[1] The essay is translated by Leonard E. Mins in *International Literature*, No. 11, Moscow, 1935.

the end of the essay he compares Nietzsche with Don Quixote, and this comparison could lead Thomas Mann to revise his whole attitude to Nietzsche and therewith to the problems of German development in the nineteenth century. In the essay itself this comparison is no more than an *aperçu*. But precisely Thomas Mann's organic development may give the reader hope that it will go beyond this.

It is understandable, indeed almost inevitable, that the anti-fascist struggle of the bourgeois humanists should begin with an attack simply on the immediate political activity of the National Socialists. Hitler's barbarism was such an unheard-of thing that, in comparison, every past stage in German development seemed an age of culture. Fascism seemed a total break with the whole of German history. But the important thinkers of the anti-fascist movement sooner or later get beyond the immediate surface and forms of fascism. This initial attitude is after all no more than a cultural rendering of the idea that both middle and working class in the Third Reich are victims of a petty-bourgeois stratum turned savage, barbaric and brutal. But once honest and percipient anti-fascists become aware of the monopoly-capitalist character of National Socialism, the way lies free for them, culturally too, to discover the connection between fascism and the reactionary tendencies of the past.

This process has begun in the last few years. The great international anti-fascist movement is therefore now beginning to address its criticism to capitalist culture in general, and to that of the imperialist period in particular. And here and there a critical attitude is being adopted towards thinkers who were formerly blindly admired, but in whom reactionary tendencies, leading to fascism, are now becoming evident. The most important representatives of the anti-fascist front are now engaged on this revision of their ideological equipment; amongst them Thomas Mann. Therefore, if he is quicker to take a stand on immediate political issues than to reassess the past philosophically and historically, this should not be surprising. On the contrary, one should see in this a healthy pointer to development. For to understand relationships of the past correctly, a correct creative attitude to the present is a necessary preliminary.

Mann's essays which we have discussed here should also be viewed in this context of transition. If we have measured their methods and conclusions against certain much more progressive statements of their author, we do not forget that the majority of these essays were written before Hitler's seizure of power and that since then Thomas Mann has travelled a long way. Our only wish is—in the interests of the anti-fascist struggle and of German culture—that Thomas Mann himself should become more aware of this distance and that that fine organic relationship between all his views should constellate round his most advanced.

1936

Appendix C

THE LAST GREAT CRITICAL REALIST

HARDLY two months have passed since the whole cultural world celebrated the eightieth birthday of Thomas Mann, the last great representative of critical realism. Today all true men of culture, all true humanists unite at his grave in mourning and pain. The sense of loss is deepened by the fact that Thomas Mann's vast *oeuvre* was far from complete in his eightieth year. About a year ago there appeared the continuation of his fragmentary youthful work *Confessions of Felix Krull, Confidence Man*, demonstrating to the delight and amazement of millions of his readers that a grand, humorous novel with a contemporary theme was still possible in our time. Unfortunately, this book remains in all probability a fragment. The eighty-year-old Thomas Mann died at the height of his powers, in the midst of his work.

His ability to defy old-age, to keep pace with the development of the world is a decisive feature of Mann's literary personality. Despite, or because of, the very perfection of his work, he has never indulged in experiment for the sake of form. On the contrary, content and form have always been engendered by the author's inner conflicts, by his struggle with the great problems of his time. It is this oneness with the problems of the epoch, this fresh receptivity for everything new, everything pointing to the future, that provides the key to Mann's ever-young literary personality.

The history of our epoch travels along complicated and intri-

cate paths. Mann's career, therefore, reflecting these paths and
their perspectives, could not be straightforward. Especially as
he was and remained a bourgeois writer; it was no light, easily
accomplished task, therefore, for him to overcome certain
bourgeois prejudices. Admittedly, right from the beginning
Mann was a bourgeois writer who understood the predicaments
of the bourgeoisie in his time. But the young Thomas Mann
could only oppose to the cultural poverty and inhumanity of
capitalism the culture and humanism of a former bourgeois-
patrician past (e.g., his world-famous novel *Buddenbrooks* and
his early stories). Thus he could only criticize the capitalist
system from the standpoint of a romantic anti-capitalist; a criticism therefore which inevitably lacked perspective. Hence it is
not surprising that Thomas Mann was pulled along by the
current of the First World War.

But this aberration did not last long. With the collapse of
Hohenzollern Germany and the rise of the Weimar Republic
Thomas Mann took his place in the struggle for a democratic
development. He was one of the first writers to recognize the
danger of the new, emerging type of reaction, fascism, and to
take issue with it courageously at the highest literary level. This
ideological struggle forms the axis of his novel *The Magic
Mountain*. The story *Mario and the Magician* is already a frontal
attack upon fascist demagogy.

In this story the outlook of the mature Thomas Mann emerges
with particular clarity. One character, a gentleman from Rome,
resists the fascist 'spellbinding', the mass hypnosis, yet sur-
renders in the end. The reason for his collapse is, as Thomas
Mann shows artistically, the purely negative character of his
resistance. The mere rejection of fascist inhumanity, however
well-intentioned, is a wasted gesture: merely to say 'no' is
powerless and foredoomed. To the mendacious pseudo-ideals of
fascism we must oppose genuine, well-founded ideals, if we really
want the good cause to triumph; which means, in regard to

literature, that without a positive perspective no effective realist literature can exist.

His grasp of social life, his active participation in social struggles led Thomas Mann to see this perspective in socialism. Not that he was ever a socialist; Thomas Mann was and remained a bourgeois. But as a great man and a great writer he realized that the contradictions of bourgeois society could only be solved by socialism; that only socialism could prevent mankind from sinking into barbarism. And since he was able to give genuine artistic expression to this awareness, his social pictures could never be pessimistic, however unsparingly he exposed the insuperable contradictions of bourgeois life in his epoch. It suffices if we think of the closing scene of his *Faustus* to see this connection clearly.

In Thomas Mann's artistic development man and writer combine in a militant unity. Everyone knows Mann's contribution to the ideological struggle against Hitler; everyone knows of his courageous and resolute stand over the years for peace, against atomic warfare, for the peaceful, democratic reunification of the German people. But perhaps not everyone understands that these social problems go to the very core of Mann's literary work. We are not dealing with a world-famous man whose social concerns and utterances are simply a matter of conscience, existing, as it were, alongside and in relative independence of his writing. No, the crown to Mann's development is the merging of these two centres, that of his creative work with that of his philosophical and political struggles. It is this unity which has given such force and conviction to his public statements. And it is the secret to the power of his work.

Thomas Mann occupies a special position in the history of critical realism. While the great bourgeois realists, say from Fielding to Tolstoy, presented bourgeois life itself, Thomas Mann gives us a totality of the inner problems of contemporary bourgeois life. Obviously not in an abstract, conceptual form; Mann always presents living people and real situations. However, the particular position he takes vis-à-vis the present and future of bourgeois society makes him choose his characters and plots from the standpoint of these inner problems rather than directly from everyday life. Thus the class struggle between proletariat and bourgeoisie is not reflected immediately in his work. But the ideological, emotional and moral problems, all the typical reflexes of bourgeois society upon which class struggle leaves its mark emerge as a result in a more complete, more comprehensive totality. In this sense Thomas Mann is as much the great historian of life in bourgeois society as Balzac or Stendhal. Posterity will be able to recapture from his work with equal freshness how the typical figures of present-day bourgeois society lived, with what issues they wrestled, as they will the more distant past from the work of the great critical realists.

But beyond that Thomas Mann's literary qualities have a peculiarly topical significance. His problems, in a modified form, are those of millions of middle-class people, millions of human beings who have grown up and are living under the influence of a bourgeois outlook. The questions and answers posed in his works are the most suitable for confronting these people with a choice: between war and peace, humanity and inhumanity, in the final analysis—between capitalism and socialism. Thomas Mann not only faces them with this choice, but also shows them the path they must take. For this reason Thomas Mann is not only the greatest bourgeois writer of his time, but at the same time, and inseparably therefrom, a great educator of society in his time, in the same way as his literary ancestors, the great critical realists.

13th August, 1955.

INDEX

Titles of works mentioned in the text are listed under name of author. Figures in italics indicate more detailed treatment.

STUDIES IN EUROPEAN REALISM

by GEORG LUKÁCS

with an introduction by ALFRED KAZIN

Little known in the United States, the name of Georg Lukács carries an almost legendary prestige in European intellectual circles. Writers and thinkers of such differing outlooks as Thomas Mann, Herbert Read, Jean-Paul Sartre, and Karl Mannheim have saluted Lukács' theoretical work—in literary criticism, philosophy, esthetics, and the sociology of knowledge—as towering contributions. Born in Hungary in 1885, Lukács studied in Germany and was influenced by Hegel, Max Weber, and, finally, by the early philosophical writings of Marx. His Marxism, as it developed, was a singularly paradoxical and idiosyncratic doctrine—shaped by an eminent sense of the humanist tradition and charged with an overriding concern for the problems of individualism and alienation—and Lukács has, over the years, been continuously under attack by the Communist orthodoxy.

Studies in European Realism represents Lukács' critical vision in its richest and most brilliant expression. "Which of the two," he asks, "Balzac or Flaubert, was the greatest novelist of the 19th century? . . . Does the modern novel reach its culminating point in Gide, Proust, and Joyce or had it already reached its peak much earlier in Balzac and Tolstoy?" These are questions that, rather than relying on mere matters of taste for an answer, involve all the central problems of the novel as an art form. And Lukács, drawing upon the vast resource of classical European culture, answers them in vigorous extended essays that refer the reader back to the development of literature, if not culture itself, as a whole.

". . . *Studies in European Realism* is an important landmark for all twentieth-century students of the novel."

—Harry Levin

UL *166* $*1.95*

History and Political Science

Literature, Criticism, Drama, and Poetry

Psychology

Titles of General Interest